KNOW, BELIEVE, & LIVE THE TRUTH OF WHO YOU ARE

IDENTITY RESTORATION

RAY LEIGHT

Identity Restoration: Know, Believe, & Live the Truth of Who You Are
Copyright © 2017 by Raymond Leight

Requests for information should be addressed to: info@obedienceofbelief.org

Cover Design: Robert Schwendenmann (bobbyhere@gmail.com)
Cover Art: KW www.instagram.com/paperandpomes
Interior Layout and Formatting: Robert Schwendenmann
Editors: Ashley Read (ashleybread@gmail.com), Melissa Daumont
(melissa.daumont512@gmail.com), and Kathryn Leight

ISBN-10: 0-9966989-2-2
ISBN-13: 978-09966989-2-4

Please note that the author's publishing style capitalizes certain pronouns in Scripture that refer to Father, Son, Holy Spirit and may differ from other publishers' styles.

IDENTITY RESTORATION

KNOW, BELIEVE, & LIVE THE TRUTH OF WHO YOU ARE

TABLE OF CONTENTS

DEDICATION

I would like to dedicate this book to all the people who refuse to accept the "less than" kingdom lifestyle. Those who have had the courage to face their issues, their lies, and their disbelief, and pursue freedom. For all the groundbreakers who went before me, helping to make this book possible. Without all of the courageous people throughout church history, who chose freedom and then shared their insights and revelations, this book may have never happened. I dedicate this book to all of those before me who have cut a path for freedom and to all of those who will continue.

ACKNOWLEDGEMENTS

I want to truly thank all of those who have challenged me throughout the years of my walk with the Lord. This book would not have the Scriptural foundation and insights in it, if I had not been challenged and questioned at the level I have been. It hasn't always been fun, but it sure has been fruitful. Thank you!

I also want to thank my wife, Kathryn. You have never allowed me to compromise, and you have always been there encouraging me and believing in me. Your opinion matters. I love you!

NOTES FROM THE AUTHOR

The concept of "Identity Restoration" is the expression of many years of study, discipleship, mentoring, pastoring, inner healing, personal revelation, and individual growth. My wife and I started our journey with the Lord back in 1996. The inner healing focus has refined our mission of equipping disciples and has accelerated people's growth into living out the truth of who they are in Christ. This book will walk you through some of the Scriptures, personal revelations, and testimonies of how to live a practical and sustainable kingdom lifestyle of freedom and healing. Enjoy and be free!

Restore us to Yourself, O LORD, that we may be restored! Renew our days as of old.

– Lamentations 5:21

HOW DID YOU GET INTO THIS?

My wife, Kathryn, and I get asked a lot of questions when we are traveling and ministering. One of the most common questions is something similar to this: "How did you get into this ministry?" My usual answer to that question is, "I needed it." This is the story of my journey.

I didn't grow up with any real understanding of God or faith. I was a very confused child in a very broken family. At a young age, I started looking for any creative way to numb the emotional pain I was experiencing. When I was 10, I remember a specific moment when I shut down my emotions. They were of no good use to me. By the time I was 15, I was in a very dark place, involved with behaviors and activities that I should not have been involved with. I was so empty by then that when one of the things I was holding on to for a sense of purpose fell apart, I attempted suicide. Fortunately, I was not successful. At that point in my life, my apathy was so strong that I wasn't even inspired to try again when the first attempt failed. From there I stumbled along in life, wounded and empty, with no desire for or knowledge of God. During that time, I didn't really have any examples of Christianity that represented anything that was helpful to my life. I mocked the whole idea of God.

Fast forward to when I was 30. I was married to Kathryn and we had our two children by then. Our daughter was six, and our son was one. Kathryn had recently come to know Jesus. Though she came to know Him in a very powerful way, it didn't really affect me. If she needed that crutch and it helped, good for her. I just didn't think I needed it. At one point around that time while I was alone in our bedroom, I proposed a challenge to the Lord. I spoke out to Him, "If You are real, reveal Yourself to me. Otherwise, I am just talking to myself." Then I went on with my day.

That was it. That was the extent of my prayer. Well, a few weeks later I experienced what I now know to be a vision. I still remember it, and can feel it, like it happened yesterday. In the vision, I was standing in the doorway of my dad's office that was in the basement of my childhood home. The room was completely empty. There was no furniture, bookshelves, or anything that had actually been in his office. Another odd thing was that there was a large fireplace on the wall across from me with a fire burning in it. This was odd because there was no fireplace in my dad's old office. I stood there, a little bewildered, and wondering why I was there. Then, as I looked over at the fire in the fireplace, it started to move. It began to grow and come out of the fireplace. The different flames of the fire began to extend and reach for me like fingers on a hand. That moment still brings chills to me. That is the moment when it all made sense. I could feel the fires of hell reaching for me and I began to understand what that meant for me. As the fire was growing and it began to come toward me, fear rose up in me. Just before the hand of flames reached me, I called out to Jesus. I didn't even understand why I knew to do that. I just did it. When I did, He came to me. He entered into the vision from behind and above me on my right side. As He drew near, the fire and the rest of the vision faded until it was all just the brightness of His presence. Once I was overtaken by His presence and the fear was gone, I came out of the vision and was back in our bedroom—the same room I had been in just a few weeks ago, when I flippantly asked God to reveal Himself to me. My life changed significantly after that. One of the first tangible differences I noticed was that I could read. I was dyslexic growing up and had trouble reading anything. Not only that, but I discovered that the Scriptures were no longer dry, boring information to me. They actually brought life, and it was amazing.

Kathryn and I started a life of faith and soon felt called to pursue a deeper lifestyle of faith. We really wanted to make an impact in our children's lives and leave a legacy of authenticity and love for them. We attended an event from Family Life Ministries called "I Still Do" and were inspired to join the staff of Campus Crusade for Christ (CRU). We started that process in 2001 and eventually became missionaries with one of their ministries, Life Builders. We learned an incredible amount during this time, and spent several years working with individuals and couples in relational mentoring and discipleship. Over and over again we would walk people through a process of discovering their value, purpose, and identity in Christ.

As I mentioned, my life significantly changed when I came to faith, though I still had a lot of hurts, wounds, and lies I was carrying with me from my old life. I didn't realize how much I was carrying until our daughter decided she wanted to go back to public school for tenth grade. She had been home schooled since third grade and now wanted to go to school with her friends. In the summer of 2005 while Kathryn and I were at the "Meet the Teachers" night, I had a simple thought that started a landslide in my heart. As we were there I remember thinking, "This isn't that difficult. It wouldn't have been that difficult for my parents to be involved in my life." Over the next few weeks, that simple thought turned into anger, and then resentment. Then something happened. It felt like my heart had been ripped open and all of those emotions I packed away when I was ten came flooding out. I was experiencing emotional pain with the intensity of a startling adrenaline rush. This drove me into a deep depression. I began to have trouble with basic relational interaction and simple tasks. It got so bad that I even had trouble driving, and sometimes Kathryn had to drive me places.

During this time a friend of mine recommended that I pray with one of his friends. He told me that his friend meets with people and helps them to connect their head and their heart[1]. His friend wasn't local, and if I was going to pray with him, I would have to travel to another state. I didn't understand why I had to travel and pray with someone. I had been praying and it didn't work. Why would praying with someone else matter? I reluctantly agreed to go and eventually traveled six hours to meet with him. Honestly, I was throwing a complete fit on the trip down. I had no faith for this process. I had already planned on going to a counselor and getting on medication for the depression when I came back. I am not even sure why I agreed to go, except maybe that I had nothing to lose.

While I was there an amazing thing happened. I experienced the love of Jesus and the power of the cross. In an encounter with Jesus, I was reconciled to myself and the woman my mother was created to be. It was life changing and revelatory. I can't even fully describe the transformation that happened. One of the most amazing changes that happened was the depression was gone, completely gone. I was totally set free from the overwhelming weight and depression that had been debilitating me. The freedom I received during this time was truly amazing. It was not the end of my journey, it was more like the beginning. Even though I had come to faith nine years earlier, this started an intentional pursuit of freedom that was fresh and new. I found there was so much more freedom and healing available. I have had so much healing since then, and I am still pursuing more. I have been delivered from an addiction to negativity, set free from a mindset of rejection, and have been released from a lifestyle of rebellion. This healing has come through many forms – through personal encounters with God, visions, prayer times, Scripture reading, listening to sermons, worship, teachings, prophetic words, and conversations with friends.

On the drive home from the initial prayer time, I remember thinking, "If I can be healed, anybody can be healed." This started the journey of discovery and revelation of inner healing. During this process, Kathryn and I have also been able to help others on their journey. Taking personal responsibility for our own thoughts and feelings and continuing our journey was not always easy. It is not always fun to acknowledge an area of your life that doesn't represent the truth of the Gospel, and confront it. But we chose to not compromise and accept "better" as "complete." Like I mentioned, I received a deep revelation in that first prayer time, although after the dust settled, I realized there was more freedom available. We now live a lifestyle of continual pursuit of the righteousness, peace, and joy that is the kingdom of God.

Before going for prayer, it was recommended that I read one of Leanne Payne's[2] books called *Crisis in Masculinity*. This resource was the beginning of my research in this subject. Many ministries, books, and hours of research later, I heard about Dawna De Silva and Teresa Liebscher's Sozo[3] ministry. I began to study and practice it with people. I saw how beneficial it could be to help someone interact with the Lord, be set free from their lies and wounds, and receive truth. It was so much easier and more effective than slowly trying to convince someone of truth week after week. It was amazing how it accelerated the discipleship process.

We were called from the very beginning of our faith walk to bring generational change to people's lives. This additional tool helped us refine that calling and become more effective in that purpose. In 2009 we were inspired to establish Faith by Grace Ministries[4]. This has allowed us to help equip generations of disciples into a practical and sustainable lifestyle of freedom and healing. We have had the honor of watching the Lord bring freedom and healing to people who have experienced some of the worst brokenness, woundedness, abuse, and pain.

Keep in mind, inner healing prayer is a tool that works with discipleship for a lifestyle of freedom and healing. In my journey, I have refined it to be part of my personal discipleship process. This tool helps me to find out what I actually believe, and then be able to repent and receive truth. There have been many times I have had to face the reality that even though I knew the truth, I believed and was living out something different. I have had multiple sessions over the years with others helping me, as well as on my own. During this discipleship process, the Lord has used many people, experiences, teachings, encounters, and ministries to reveal to us and develop the concept of "Identity Restoration."

This concept has become a transformative movement that is helping people go from a lifestyle of fear, shame, and guilt into a lifestyle of righteousness, peace, and joy.

In the following chapters we will look at the different aspects of that lifestyle.

Endnotes:

1.   verbenafoundation.org
2.   ministriesofpastoralcare.com
3.   bethelsozo.com
4.   faithbygrace.org

CHAPTER TWO

WHAT IS IDENTITY RESTORATION?

To understand Identity Restoration, we need to start with an understanding of two things. What is our identity and what does restoration actually mean? The restoration part is easy. A simple online search[1] will reveal that restoration is: *the act of returning something to a former owner, place, or condition; the act of bringing back something that existed before; the act of returning something that was stolen or taken.* The identity part might be a little more complicated for some. This is where it gets interesting. What is our identity and how can it be restored?

In my understanding of Scripture, the truth of who we are is already true. We are not in the process of becoming who we are created to be. We already are who God created us to be. We are in the process of believing who God created us to be. We don't presently look and act like who we really are because we don't believe it. Of course, part of that process of believing who we are must include believing in our Creator. To be able to know who you are in Christ begins with believing in

Jesus Christ. We will look at this process more clearly in the following chapters. If you want to start with a foundational understanding of the truth of who you are in Christ, I recommend that you experience my Bible study called *Who Do You Think You Are?*[2] This two-volume study is a comprehensive breakdown of several hundred aspects of your identity in Christ that you explore in hundreds of Scriptures in context. That study will complement this book in a way that will increase your understanding and ability to know, believe, and live the truth of who you are.

"Identity Restoration is the act of returning the truth of who you are in Christ, to you."

With that understanding of identity and restoration, here is a definition. Identity Restoration is the act of returning the truth of who you are in Christ, to you. It is the process of taking back from the enemy what he has stolen, and allowing yourself to take ownership of your restored, true identity. This is what we help people do in our workshops, teachings, coaching, and individual healing sessions.

Again, the truth of who you are is already true. We are not creating any new truth. Revelation of truth comes from the Holy Spirit through spiritual discernment.

> The natural person does not accept the things of the Spirit of God, for they are folly to him, and he is not able to understand them because they are spiritually discerned.
> – 1 Corinthians 2:14

> Now to Him who is able to strengthen you according to my gospel and the preaching of Jesus Christ, according to the

revelation of the mystery that was kept secret for long ages.
– Romans 16:25

Revelation – the Greek word used here is *apokalyptō* (Strong's G601). It means: to reveal, lay bare, or disclose truth that was previously unknown.

An expression of the Scripture including the fullness of that definition could be:

> *Now to Him who is able to strengthen you according to my gospel and the preaching of Jesus Christ, according to the truth and the mystery that He has revealed, laid bare, and disclosed that was previously unknown and kept secret for long ages.*

So remember, there is no new truth. The Holy Spirit is just revealing truth to us that is already true. We just didn't know it or believe it.

In John 16, the Scripture tells us Jesus sent the Holy Spirit to guide us into all truth. It also tells us Jesus is glorified when the Holy Spirit reveals truth to us. Having the truth of who you are in Christ revealed

---

> *"When we know and believe the truth, we will live the truth."*

---

to you actually glorifies Jesus. Take the time right now to read John 16:1-15 and consider that before moving on.

Once the Holy Spirit reveals the truth, we have the opportunity to believe that truth. When we know and believe the truth, we will live the truth. This is the life of faith – knowing and believing that it is no longer our old self that is living. It is Christ who lives in us. The life we live now we live by faith in Jesus, who loved us and gave Himself for us.

To help understand the Identity Restoration process that will be explained later, here is a brief overview of who God created us to be, how the enemy stole that from us, and how Jesus restored us back to who God created us to be.

ORIGINAL CREATION

In the beginning, God created the heavens and the earth. – Genesis 1:1

In the beginning was the Word, and the Word was with God, and the Word was God. He was in the beginning with God. All things were made through Him, and without Him was not any thing made that was made. In Him was life, and the life was the light of men. The light shines in the darkness, and the darkness has not overcome it. – John 1:1-5

And God saw everything that He had made, and behold, it was very good. – Genesis 1:31

Throughout the first chapter of Genesis, while God was narrating the original creation, He would stop and see that it was good. Everything He created was good. When He finished, He stopped and beheld that everything He had made was very good. His original intent for us was to be very good. I don't believe it was ever His intention for us to sin and fall from grace. Unfortunately, that is what happened.

THE FALL

In the third chapter of Genesis, the very good went very bad. This is where the enemy came in and deceived Adam and Eve. The beginning of Chapter Three starts with:

> Now the serpent was more crafty than any other beast of the field that the LORD God had made. He said to the woman, "Did God actually say, 'You shall not eat of any tree in the garden'?" – Genesis 3:1

This type of deception started it all. The enemy is the father of lies. He introduced doubt and confusion by questioning what the Lord had said. The enemy is still using this same style of deception to destroy the identity and authority of the church. "Did God actually say?" has transformed in modern day to things like "Can you really be sure that was God talking to you?" This deception has influenced many in the church to believe the lie: "You can't know for sure that you are hearing from the Lord." This lie, in its multiple variations, is one of the two lies that I believe to be the most pervasive and destructive lies attacking the church today. We will talk about the second lie in Chapter Three.

The deception introduced in the garden led to the beginning of sin and the eating of the fruit from the tree of the knowledge of good and evil. From there the destruction continued and spread to all men. That is how our identity was stolen by the enemy, and he is still lying to us.

THE CROSS

Thankfully God did what the law was unable to do. By sending His own Son in the likeness of sinful flesh and for sin, He condemned sin in the flesh. Our old selves were crucified with Jesus in order that the body of sin might be brought to nothing and the righteous requirement of the law might be fulfilled in us. To those who received Him, who believed in His name, He gave the right to become children of God. We are no longer enslaved to sin. He made all things new. This is how He restored us back to our originally intended, very good, identity.

In the rest of the chapters we will look at the process of restoration.

"We are no longer enslaved to sin."

We will look at our guaranteed inheritance of righteousness, peace, and joy, how the enemy tries to steal that from us, and how to live a lifestyle of freedom and healing. Some of the chapters will have a practical application to bring personal transformation and restoration.

PRACTICAL APPLICATION

For this practical application we are going to review some of the Scriptures we looked at in this chapter and allow you to work out what you believe about them. Read the following sections of Scripture and then fill in the blanks with the specifics. This application is intended to stir up your sincere minds with reminding you of these truths (2 Peter 3:1). I am using the ESV version for this exercise. This will work with other versions, but if you do not have the ESV and would like to use an online version, one available resource is the Blue Letter Bible[3].

Read John 16:1-15

John 16:7

Nevertheless, I tell you the truth:_____

_____, for

if I do not go away, the Helper will not come to you. But if I go,

_____.

John 16:8

And when He comes, He will convict the world concerning

_____:

John 16:9-11

concerning sin, because they do not believe in Me; concerning

_____, because I go to the Father, _____

_____; concerning judgment,

because the ruler of this world is judged.

John 16:13

When the Spirit of truth comes,_____

_____, for He will

not speak on His own authority, but whatever He hears He will

speak, and He will declare to you the things that are to come.

John 16:14-15

He will _____, for He will take what is Mine

and _____. All that the Father

has is Mine; therefore I said that_____

_____

Now that you have read the Scripture and filled in the corresponding blanks, review these kingdom concepts and ask God:

"What truths about my identity, according to those Scriptures, do You want me to know?"

_____

_____

_____

_____

_____

Let yourself think, imagine, or dream, and ask God: "How could believing these truths affect my life?"

_____

_____

_____

_____

_____

Ask God: "What are some practical steps I can take to experience these truths in my life?"

_____

_____

_____

_____

_____

Now ask the Holy Spirit to empower you and make these truths more real in your life.

Endnotes:

1. dictionary.com
2. faithbygrace.org/resources
3. blueletterbible.org

CHAPTER THREE

NEW CREATION

n this chapter we are going to look at who God says we were, what happened to change that, and who we are now.

THE OLD SELF

You don't have to look far to see who we were. This is something we are very familiar with. Following are two of the most common Scriptures used to point to the old self.

> The heart is deceitful above all things, and desperately sick; who can understand it? – Jeremiah 17:9

> As it is written: "None is righteous, no, not one; no one understands; no one seeks for God. All have turned aside; together they have become worthless; no one does good, not even one." – Romans 3:10-12

Along with these two Scriptures, here is quick overview of our old identity without Christ. We were:

deceitful – desperately sick – wicked – unrighteous – not understanding – not seeking God – worthless – not good – dead in sin and trespasses – disobedient – separate – alienated – hopeless – without God – far off – hostile – sold under sin – a slave to sin – nothing good dwelling in us – sin dwelling in us.

This isn't even a comprehensive list. Needless to say, we had a problem. What we must keep in mind is that when the Scriptures reveal these things, they say that we once *were* those things. They are not saying we are those things.

WHAT HAPPENED?

Here is one of the more well-known Scriptures about what happened:

For God so loved the world, that He gave His only Son, that whoever believes in Him should not perish but have eternal life. For God did not send His Son into the world to condemn the world, but in order that the world might be saved through Him. – John 3:16-17

What happened? Jesus happened! The good news happened!

Let's look at two Scriptures, and a couple of Greek words, to help us understand this good news.

We know that our old self was crucified with Him in order that the body of sin might be brought to nothing, so that we would no longer be enslaved to sin. For one who has died has been set free from sin. – Romans 6:6

The word "nothing" in this Scripture, as you will see in the definition following, pretty much means "nothing."

Nothing – the Greek word used here is *katargeō* (Strong's G2673). It means: to be entirely idle – to render useless, abolish, cease, cumber, deliver, destroy, do away, become of no effect, fail, loose, bring to nought, put away, put down, vanish away, make void.

In Him also you were circumcised with a circumcision made without hands, by putting off the body of the flesh, by the circumcision of Christ. – Colossians 2:11

Putting off – the Greek used here is *apekdysis* (Strong's G555). It means: a putting off – laying aside.

An expression of these two Scriptures, together with the expanded definitions from the Greek, could be:

Your old self was crucified, and your body of sin has been brought to nothing – rendered useless, abolished, destroyed, made void, caused to cease, done away with, become of no effect, and loosed from you. The old body of flesh has been circumcised in Christ and has been put off and laid aside.

When we repented and put our faith in Jesus, that actually happened. It is real. Praise God!

WHO WE ARE

Before we move on to who we are now, we need to re-address Jeremiah 17:9. In my experience, this Scripture is one of the most common Scriptures taken out of context to deny the work of Jesus on the cross. I don't understand it, but I commonly get challenged with this Scripture when I am speaking about our identity in Christ. It is brought up as a challenge and a rebuttal of our new identity in Christ.

It is sad that so many Christians are so well trained to refute the gospel. You may have heard it said before that your heart is wicked and you cannot trust it. This is so commonly shared as an absolute because that is what the Scripture says.

> The heart is deceitful above all things, and desperately sick (ESV & NASB), desperately wicked (NKJ), beyond a cure (NIV), who can know and understand it? – Jeremiah 17:9

"It is sad that so many Christians are so well trained to refute the gospel."

I am not diminishing or denying this Scripture in any way. The Old Testament absolutely does say this, though you don't even need to go to the New Testament to see that something changed. All you need to do is keep reading the Old Testament. Further along in Jeremiah, God shares about the New Covenant, and then in Ezekiel, God tells us directly what He did because of this heart problem.

> Behold, the days are coming, declares the LORD, when I will make a new covenant with the house of Israel and the house of Judah, not like the covenant that I made with their

fathers on the day when I took them by the hand to bring them out of the land of Egypt, My covenant that they broke, though I was their husband, declares the LORD. For this is the covenant that I will make with the house of Israel after those days, declares the LORD: I will put My law within them, and I will write it on their hearts. And I will be their God, and they shall be My people. – Jeremiah 31:31-33

And I will give them one heart, and a new spirit I will put within them. I will remove the heart of stone from their flesh and give them a heart of flesh, that they may walk in My statutes and keep My rules and obey them. And they shall be My people, and I will be their God.
– Ezekiel 11:19-20

I will take you from the nations and gather you from all the countries and bring you into your own land. I will sprinkle clean water on you, and you shall be clean from all your uncleannesses, and from all your idols I will cleanse you. And I will give you a new heart, and a new spirit I will put within you. And I will remove the heart of stone from your flesh and give you a heart of flesh. And I will put My Spirit within you, and cause you to walk in My statutes and be careful to obey My rules. – Ezekiel 36:24-27

To believe, as a born-again child of God, that you are still just a sinner with a wicked heart is the second of those two destructive lies I mentioned in Chapter Two. Yes, our hearts were desperately sick, wicked, and beyond a cure. There was no cure for that heart. That is why God had to remove that heart and give us a new one. He has given us a new, clean heart and a new, clean spirit so that we can walk in His truth.

"He has given us a new, clean heart and a new, clean spirit so that we can walk in His truth."

Therefore, if anyone is in Christ, he is a new creation. The old has passed away; behold, the new has come. All this is from God, who through Christ reconciled us to Himself and gave us the ministry of reconciliation.
– 2 Corinthians 5:17-18

Who are we? We are a new creation with a new heart. The old heart is gone, the new has come. All this is from God, who through Christ reconciled us to Himself.

But thanks be to God, that you who were once slaves of sin have become obedient from the heart to the standard of teaching to which you were committed, and, having been set free from sin, have become slaves of righteousness.
– Romans 6:17-18

For God has done what the law, weakened by the flesh, could not do. By sending His own Son in the likeness of sinful flesh and for sin, He condemned sin in the flesh, in order that the righteous requirement of the law might be fulfilled in us, who walk not according to the flesh but according to the Spirit. – Romans 8:3-4

In Ezekiel, the Lord tells us that He gave us a new heart. In Jeremiah, He tells us that He wrote the law on that new heart. Then in Romans, He tells us that the righteous requirement of the law is fulfilled in that new heart. That is an amazing truth. We have been completely set free

"We have been completely set free from sin, have become slaves to righteousness, and have the righteous requirement of the law fulfilled in us."

from sin, have become slaves to righteousness, and have the righteous requirement of the law fulfilled in us. That is good news!

We are God's people with new, clean hearts. New creations, reconciled to God, and clean from all of our uncleannesses. We are slaves of righteousness, obedient from the heart, walking in the Spirit, with the righteous requirement of the law fulfilled in us.

That is who we are.

PRACTICAL APPLICATION

For this practical application we are going to review some of the Scriptures we looked at in this chapter and allow you to work out what you believe about them. Read the following sections of Scripture and then fill in the blanks with the specifics. This application is intended to stir up your sincere minds by reminding you of these truths (2 Peter 3:1). I am using the ESV version for this exercise. This will work with other versions, but if you do not have the ESV and would like to use one online, I recommend the Blue Letter Bible.[1]

Read Romans 6:1-14

Romans 6:6

We know that our old self was_____

in order that_____

_____, so that we would no longer be

enslaved to sin. For one who has died has_____

_____.

Read Ezekiel 36:22-30

Ezekiel 36:25-27

I will sprinkle clean water on you, and_____

_____,

and from all your idols _____.

And I will give you_____

_____.

And I will remove the heart of stone from your flesh and give you

_____.

And I will put_____,

and cause you to walk in My statutes and be careful to obey My rules.

Now that you have read the Scripture and filled in the corresponding blanks, review these kingdom concepts and ask God:

"What truths about my identity, according to those Scriptures, do You want me to know?"

_____

_____

_____

_____

_____

Let yourself think, imagine, or dream, and ask God: "How could believing these truths affect my life?"

_____

_____

_____

_____

_____

Ask God: "What are some practical steps I can take to experience these truths in my life?"

_____

_____

_____

_____

_____

Now ask the Holy Spirit to empower you and make these truths more real in your life.

_____

Endnotes:

1.   blueletterbible.org

CHAPTER FOUR

TWO DIFFERENT KINGDOMS

Though we are in the world, we are not of the kingdom of the world. We are children and citizens of the kingdom of God. The Lord has rescued us from the dominion of darkness, and transferred us to the kingdom of His beloved Son. In Romans 14:17, the Word tells us that God's kingdom is of righteousness, peace, and joy in the Holy Spirit. That is our guaranteed inheritance in Christ. Although this is the normal Christian life, it is not what we always experience in this world.

I have focused on the ministry of our identity in Christ for many years now. Several years ago, as I was reading Genesis, the Lord revealed something to me in the third chapter. We have already looked at the first chapter of Genesis, where everything the Lord created was very good. Something changed in the third chapter. Take the time right now to read Genesis 3:1-13 and reflect on it before moving on.

It all started with the deception from the enemy. The Lord did not lie when He told Adam and Eve that they would die if they ate of the tree. The enemy deceived them with questioning whether they really heard God right and then lied to them and told them, "You will not surely die." If you think about it, they had no concept of what a lie was. The enemy is the father of lies, and they had never experienced such a thing. All they knew was truth from God at this point, though they still had the choice to believe God, or to believe the enemy. As we all know, they made the wrong choice and that choice was to believe a lie. When they believed that lie, it manifested into eating the fruit from the tree of the knowledge of good and evil.

> *"They would have never eaten the fruit if they did not believe the lie."*

In my opinion, the real sin and the real problem was not eating of the fruit. It was believing the lie. They would have never eaten the fruit if they did not believe the lie. Eating the fruit was fully grown sin (James 1:15), though it was just a manifestation of the actual sin of believing the lie. I plan to explore and explain this further in a future book called *Obedience Of Belief*.

When they did believe the lie, several things happened. Believing the lie manifested into sinful behavior (eating the fruit), and it also manifested into systems of self-protection. They hid from God, covered themselves, and blamed someone. Let's read through Genesis 3:1-13 together and look at that more closely.

> Now the serpent was more crafty than any other beast of the field that the Lord God had made. He said to the woman, **"Did God actually say, 'You shall not eat of any tree in the garden'** (*the deceiving question*)?" And the woman said to the serpent, "We may eat of the fruit of the trees in the

garden, but God said, 'You shall not eat of the fruit of the tree that is in the midst of the garden, neither shall you touch it, lest you die.'" But the serpent said to the woman, **"You will not surely die** (*the father of lies, introducing a lie*)." For God knows that when you eat of it your eyes will be opened, and you will be like God, knowing good and evil." So when the woman saw that the tree was good for food, and that it was a delight to the eyes, and that the tree was to be desired to make one wise, **she took of its fruit and ate, and she also gave some to her husband who was with her, and he ate** (*sin manifesting into sinfulness*). Then the eyes of both were opened, and they knew that they were naked. **And they sewed fig leaves together and made themselves loincloths** (*covering themselves*). And they heard the sound of the Lord God walking in the garden in the cool of the day, **and the man and his wife hid themselves** (*hiding*) from the presence of the Lord God among the trees of the garden. But the Lord God called to the man and said to him, "Where are you?" And he said, **"I heard the sound of You in the garden, and I was afraid, because I was naked, and I hid myself** (*hiding*)." He said, "Who told you that you were naked? Have you eaten of the tree of which I commanded you not to eat?" The man said, **"The woman whom You gave to be with me, she gave me fruit of the tree, and I ate** (*blame*)." Then the Lord God said to the woman, "What is this that you have done?" The woman said, **"The serpent deceived me, and I ate** (*blame*)." – Genesis 3:1-13

These self-protections of hiding, covering, and blaming are simply fear, shame, and guilt. They hid in fear, covered themselves in shame, and blamed out of guilt. Remember that the kingdom of God is righteousness, peace, and joy in the Holy Spirit. Well, the kingdom of the world is fear, shame, and guilt in our own effort. Not only do we have to experience fear, shame, and guilt, but we are doing it all in our own effort. Any way that we are experiencing those, we are doing it ourselves – no one else is doing it for us.

This pattern of fear, shame, and guilt has been passed down through the generations to us. I have seen, over and over again, that any time someone believes a lie, it will manifest into some form of sinful fruit, as well as some form of self-protection that falls into the category of fear, shame, or guilt.

There is almost no limit to what these systems can be, except they are never the kingdom of God. There are several names for them, such as defense mechanisms or coping mechanisms. Call them whatever you want, they are a result of lies. They can be an automatic response, an emotion, a wall, a perception, an addiction, a behavior, or a complete disassociation where someone will create an alternative identity or reality. These systems are only doing what someone designed them to do based on the lie they are believing. Although these systems are sometimes destructive, they are not the real problem. The lie is the real problem.

One of the analogies I use to help people understand this is to compare it to a computer. There is an operating system, and then there are applications that are installed. These applications run over the main operating system. Regardless of what the self-protections are, each one has been individually programmed by us. People may have helped us do this, but we are still the ones who programmed them. The self-protections are just like applications that we wrote and then installed over the operating system of our hearts. At some point, there was either a traumatic event, some type of thematic issue established in our lives, or we were born into a false normal. When that happened, we believed a lie and wrote a program to protect ourselves. So now, when a circumstance, situation, person, or a familiar experience presses the right button, that application runs. It doesn't even have to check in with our heart first to get permission. When we wrote the code, we already set the priority level and gave it permission to run.

The level of sophistication of each one of these systems is different. Each one is uniquely designed to do its job of protecting us. This is why we respond to things in a way that does not always match what is happening. In reality, it is because we are not responding to the current situation. We are instead reacting with a pre-programmed response to an old situation.

I have also found that sometimes we even encrypt these systems at a level that we cannot process or deprogram on our own. This is one of the reasons why we need each other. It is always easier to recognize someone else's false normal and be able to help them, than it is to recognize our own and do something about it.

Keep in mind though, the systems themselves are only a result of the lies we believe. If the enemy can deceive us and get us to believe a lie in the aspect of our identity that is meant to express peace, we will express fear. If he can get us to believe a lie in the aspect of our identity that is meant to express joy, we will express shame. If he can get us to believe a lie in the aspect of our identity that is meant to express righteousness, we will express guilt.

The attack on our peace will directly affect our authority. The attack on our joy will directly affect our identity. And the attack on our righteousness will directly affect our community.

"The enemy's plan for your life looks like this: Steal your righteousness, peace, and joy and deceive you into a life of being alone, powerless, and hopeless."

This attack on our identity, authority, and community through shame, fear, and guilt will lead to being isolated, overwhelmed, and confused. The enemy's plan for your life looks like this: Steal your righteousness, peace, and joy and deceive you into a life of being alone, powerless, and hopeless. This leads to you having to do everything all by yourself, without the ability to do it, and without the ability to receive help. That is not abundant life.

The following is showing the possible ways our lives can degrade from righteousness, peace, and joy into misery, pain, and loneliness.

This is the kingdom of God in the power of the Holy Spirit:

| Righteousness | Peace | Joy |

This is what happens when we believe lies:

| Blaming | Hiding | Covering |

This is the kingdom of the world in our own effort:

| Guilt | Fear | Shame |

These lies and self-protections will destroy and steal your:

| Community | Authority | Identity |

This is what that can look like:

Isolated	Overwhelmed	Confused
Guilty	Angry	Helpless
Untrusting	Anxious	Depressed
Alone	Powerless	Hopeless
Must do it all myself	Unable to do it	Unable to receive

That is not what it looks like to live in the victory of what God has accomplished for us. It is not normal, and it is not something you have to put up with. Freedom is available.

In the following chapters we will look at how to go from living in the kingdom of fear, shame, and guilt into the kingdom of righteousness, peace, and joy.

PRACTICAL APPLICATION

For this practical application, you have the opportunity to think and dream about how the kingdom of God could be fully expressed in your life, without any lies. This is just an exercise for you to explore the truth of the kingdom. There are no right or wrong answers.

Take some time and review the previous chart of the kingdom of the world. Let that give you an understanding of how the lies potentially work, and then let yourself dream and explore, with God, how the truth could work in your life.

This is the kingdom of God in the power of the Holy Spirit:

Righteousness   Peace   Joy

This is what happens when we believe this truth:

_____   _____   _____

This truth will bless and empower your:

Community   Authority   Identity

This is what that can look like:

_____   _____   _____

_____   _____   _____

_____   _____   _____

_____   _____   _____

CHAPTER FIVE

THREE STEPS TO LIFE

Our desire is for people to be equipped for a practical and sustainable lifestyle of freedom. Over the years of our ministry and working with thousands of people, we have been refining this process. The Three Steps to Life are one of the outcomes of that refinement. This is a very simple, yet effective tool. I have found these three steps to be a powerful way to steward a lifestyle of freedom and authority in the world.

As we have already established, righteousness, peace, and joy is normal. When that is not what is happening for you, these are the practical steps to help you find out why.

STEP ONE - INTENTIONALLY STAY PRESENT

Step One is to intentionally stay present, mentally and emotionally. What I mean by this is to stay connected and present with yourself and your situation. This is a less common practice than you may think.

"Staying present mentally and emotionally will help you to have the capacity to remove yourself from a situation if needed."

So often, instead of living in the present moment, we will not only just live in the past or the future, but we will also choose to trigger off into some sort of self-protection in the way of fear, shame, or guilt. One of the names for self-protections is "coping mechanisms." One of the things coping mechanisms can do is keep you in a dangerous or dysfunctional situation and help you cope with it, instead of actually confronting it. Staying present mentally and emotionally will help you to have the capacity to remove yourself from a situation if needed. It will also allow you to establish boundaries and healthy communication where needed instead of perpetuating the dysfunction. There has to be intentionality to this because of the many self-protections we have established that are distracting us from being present. Often, I work with people who think they are aware and present, when in reality they are just analyzing a situation from a position of self-protection. This causes them to live an observational lifestyle instead of having the ability to truly experience their lives and relationships. Others will often experience them as distant, disconnected, or distracted. Again, that is not the kingdom of God.

STEP TWO - CHOOSE REALITY

Step Two is to choose reality. What I mean by this is to let yourself actually think your thoughts and feel your feelings. To actually acknowledge what it is you are thinking and feeling, instead of denying your thoughts or feelings and telling yourself you should or shouldn't be thinking or feeling them. The Word tells us in 2 Corinthians 10:5 to capture every thought and make it obedient to Christ. If you deny or pretend that you aren't actually thinking a particular thought, you cannot bring it into obedience. You can't capture a thought you won't let yourself think. You also cannot repent from a lie you deny you believe.

"You can't capture a thought
you won't let yourself think."

Denial of emotions does not work either. I have heard it said that you cannot trust your emotions. I think that is an absurd concept. Our emotions and feelings are not a result of the fall. They are not untrustworthy. God gave them to us, and they help us discern. I am telling you that you can 100% trust your feelings 100% of the time to tell you exactly what you are personally feeling. This denial of our feelings is part of the reason we lack freedom in our lives. Our emotions are like a spiritual nervous system. They are just reporting to us what we are sensing. Our emotions do not tell us why we are sensing what we are sensing, they only tell us what we are sensing. They are part of the discernment process. What we can't always trust is the thoughts we have connected to those feelings. Allowing ourselves to feel our feelings and think the thoughts connected to them, will enable us to capture the thought and make it obedient to Christ. Denial of these does not work. It will allow those thoughts to evade capture and run rampant through our minds, potentially causing emotional havoc.

One of the common mistakes people make is that they translate their own personal emotions as discernment for what other people are feeling, thinking, or doing. This is where it goes wrong. We cannot trust our own personal emotions to tell us that information. Our emotions are an expression of our thoughts and beliefs, not what other people are thinking and believing. We cannot just accept how we feel as an accurate read of what is happening, although we can trust those feelings to help us find out what we believe is happening. If we are personally feeling an emotion that doesn't fall in the categories of righteousness, peace, and joy, we are most likely believing a lie. A lie about God, ourselves, others, or the circumstance.

"Your bad attitudes and behaviors are not an attack from the enemy, they are a partnership with him."

I do not want to discount spiritual discernment here. We do have the ability to discern what is going on with someone else or in a situation. We can feel the information around us. However, when that information causes us to feel fear, shame, or guilt, and it starts to affect us, it is no longer just information. At that point, it has connected with a lie we believe and has become our own problem. I often see people blame an atmosphere or demonic attack for their own lies and unhealthy behavior. To help you understand this better, think about how many different radio waves are playing in any given place. You are not even aware of how many radio stations are broadcasting in an area until you turn on a radio. Once you tune into a specific station and hear the song playing, it is still just information. You can hear the information and live your life freely. But, if you engage with it and start singing and dancing to that song, it is no longer just information. It is you partnering with the song through singing and dancing. It is the same way with lies. There can be any number of lies around you at any given moment. You may not even notice them until you stop and focus on one. At that point, regardless of how the enemy is delivering that lie to you, it is still just information. But once you engage with it, and come into agreement with it, it is you that is manifesting the fruit of that lie in your own effort. Your bad attitudes and behaviors are not an attack from the enemy, they are a partnership with him.

For more information on discerning atmospheres, I recommend Dawna De Silva's book *Shifting Atmospheres*.[1]

So often, people I am working with will confuse their thoughts with their feelings and then automatically accept what they are "feeling" as discernment. I believe this is one of the reasons that emotions have such a bad reputation. If we can learn the difference between the two, we can actually discern. Then, as we acknowledge our thoughts and feelings, we can take them to the Lord and repent as needed. We will look at this process in more detail later in this chapter.

STEP THREE – CONNECT WITH GOD

Step Three is to connect with God. What I mean by this is to align yourself with the reality that God is already with you. This third step is the process of allowing yourself to acknowledge the presence of God however He is revealing Himself to you in that moment. Let yourself be in the presence of God. This will allow you to engage with the Lord and bring Him into your thoughts and feelings right in the situation or circumstance that you are actually experiencing. I realize this seems backwards. It seems to make sense that we should connect with God first and then do the rest. The problem with this is that so often we have trained ourselves to automatically trigger off into some sort of self-protection, and then try to connect with God. Some of those self-protections do not allow us to receive from the Lord. I know that sounds weird, but if that wasn't the case, we would already look and behave just like Jesus. Again, this is a process of addressing what is really happening, not what you want it to be like or think it should be like. Also, this order allows us to fall in line with Scripture. The Lord tells us in Matthew 6:33 to seek first the kingdom and His righteousness. Where is the kingdom? Think about that. Luke 17:21 tells us that the kingdom of God is in our midst. Matthew 3:2 and Mark 1:15 tell us that the kingdom of God is at hand. The kingdom of God is in you right where you are. It is not in your self-protection. These three steps will allow you to seek His kingdom and His righteousness in every situation.

> *"The kingdom of God is in you right where you are. It is not in your self-protection."*

EXAMPLE

Here is an example of this process. Remember that righteousness, peace, and joy are your guaranteed inheritance and your normal Christian life. With that in mind, think about this scenario. Let's use the example of a conversation where it seems like someone is trying to manipulate you into doing something. This is a very common form of communication in the world, so it should be easy to relate to.

There you are experiencing your day, feeling great, and then suddenly your righteousness, peace, or joy turns into shame, guilt, or fear while you are interacting with someone. At that moment, intentionally stay in the interaction mentally and emotionally. Stay presently aware of yourself, where you are, and what is happening.

Then, while you are aware of your situation, choose the reality of what you are thinking and feeling in that moment. In this situation, where it seems like someone is manipulating you, most people I coach would describe it a certain way. They would say that it feels like they are being manipulated. The problem is, that is not a feeling. That is a thought. If you take your thought and make it a feeling, you will probably never get to the actual feeling and be able to address any lies you may believe. So in this situation, you now think you are being manipulated. Staying present in the situation where you think you are being manipulated, how do you feel? If it is anything other than righteousness, peace, and joy, you may believe a lie about the situation. In reality, you could even be wrong about the manipulation. Just because you think you are being manipulated doesn't mean it is happening. Either way, whether someone is trying to manipulate you or not, doesn't even matter. What you believe about that situation is what matters. Even if someone is attempting to manipulate you, you can fully experience righteousness, peace, and joy and express your true self in the situation. If you are not experiencing the kingdom in that situation, the issue in the situation is not with the person you think is manipulating you, it is with you. For example, let's say you are experiencing a sense of fear in the conversation where you think you are being manipulated. Now that you are staying present, and choosing reality, you can bring God into what you are experiencing.

"Even if someone is attempting to manipulate you, you can fully experience righteousness , peace, and joy and express your true self in the situation."

Right there, where you think you are being manipulated and you are experiencing a feeling of fear, allow yourself to connect with the presence of God. This in and of itself can resolve the fear and allow you to return to the sense of righteousness, peace, and joy. If that resolves the issue, great! There is no need to dig any deeper. If it does not, or you find this as a pattern in your life, you can allow God to reveal to you the information you need to be free. We will review that process in the following chapters.

PRACTICAL APPLICATION

In this practical application, we are going to practice the three steps. If you are comfortable where you are, try this right now. If not, get yourself to a place where you feel safe to try this. I recommend that you start out practicing this in a place where you feel safe and comfortable. There is no wrong way to do this. It is just a simple exercise to help you become aware of yourself and your surroundings.

1) Intentionally stay present

Take a moment and allow yourself to become aware of your surroundings.

Where are you?

>   Pay attention to your actual location.

>   Are you in a room, outside, a park, a beach, etc.?

>   What is around you?

What do you hear?

>   If you are in a room, what noises are in that room?

>   What noises are outside of the room?

>   What noises are around you?

>   If you are outside, what noises are you aware of?

What is the temperature?

Is it cold, cool, warm, or hot?

What can you sense physically?

Pay attention to your body.

Are you sitting?

Are you standing?

Are you lying down?

What do you physically feel?

Can you feel a breeze, the sun, etc.?

This is a process of allowing you to be present in your body and in your situation. Let yourself actually be present where you are.

2) Choose reality

Now that you are aware of your surroundings and are present in your situation, what are your thoughts and feelings?

Take a moment and let yourself become aware of the thoughts and impressions running through your mind. What are you thinking?

Are there a lot of thoughts running through your mind?

Does your mind seem blank?

Do you see anything in your mind's eye?

Are you remembering anything in particular?

Now that you are aware of your thoughts, take a moment and allow yourself to experience your feelings. Start out with just simple feelings.

Are you happy?

Are you sad?

Are you angry?

Are you afraid?

Now that you know your thoughts and are aware of your feelings, let's move on.

3) Connect with God

There are many ways you can experience the presence of God. You can feel Him, sense Him, see Him, or know that He is with you. However it is comfortable for you, allow yourself to acknowledge and be in the presence of the Lord.

Let us draw near with a true heart in full assurance of faith, with our hearts sprinkled clean from an evil conscience and our bodies washed with pure water. – Hebrews 10:22

Draw near to God, and He will draw near to you.
– James 4:8

Just allow yourself to experience the presence of God and enjoy the peace and glory. Practice this as much as you can. It will be truly beneficial for you.

Again, there is no pressure to get this right. If you can easily do this, great! If not, this may just be new for you, or you may believe lies about yourself or God, and your heart won't let you experience this. It is okay, we can get that information in the next few chapters. Slowing ourselves down and really paying attention to what is going on inside ourselves is not easy for everyone, and sometimes takes practice.

Endnotes:

1.   dawnadesilva.com

CHAPTER SIX

HEART INVENTORY

would be the first to tell you that I have no idea what is really going on inside someone's heart. We have been ministering to people for over 15 years and have been focusing more and more on the heart every year. I don't fully understand how we do what we do in our hearts, but I know it is happening. Somehow we compartmentalize information and experiences in a way that causes us to respond to things differently. In Isaiah 61:1 the Lord declares that Jesus was sent to bind up the brokenhearted. He has accomplished this. Jesus glorified the Father by completing the work the Father gave Him to do. Our broken hearts have been restored and made whole. We are not broken. But, even though we are whole in Christ, we do not always live as though we are whole. We do not fully believe we are whole. The brokenness in our thoughts, imaginations, and our beliefs affects our lives. We tend to live an inconsistent life where the circumstances and people around us seem to influence our emotions and responses in an unhealthy way.

If you remember from Chapter Four, righteousness, peace, and joy are the normal Christian life. Fear, shame, and guilt are perversions of that truth and are a direct result of lies we believe. Anywhere we are hiding in fear, covering ourselves with shame, and blaming others, we are believing lies about God, ourselves, or others.

An inventory of your heart will help you find out what you actually believe in those different areas of your heart where you are not manifesting the truth of your identity in Christ. Remember, the truth of who you are is already true. Taking inventory of your heart will help you to find out that truth, as well as the lies you believe. Not only can you find out the truth and lies, but you can find out what systems of self-protection are manifesting because of the lies. You are also able to find out what you could have if you didn't believe the lies, and if you didn't believe you had to protect yourself.

Those four simple pieces of information (truth, lies you believe, systems of self-protection you use, and what you could have instead) can help you to know who you truly are and be empowered with the information you need to be able to choose to live a victorious kingdom lifestyle.

> *"One of the key factors to experiencing God's presence is to allow yourself to be present."*

In Chapter Two, we looked at how the Holy Spirit glorifies Jesus by revealing to us the truth of who we are. Allowing the Holy Spirit to reveal that truth to us, by taking inventory of our heart, is a way of allowing Jesus to be glorified. Depending on the particular lies we believe and the self-protections we are using, we don't always allow ourselves to hear that truth. If that is your situation, I recommend praying with someone who can help you (James 5:16).

In the previous chapter, we looked at the Three Steps to Life. That process will help you be in the presence of God in your situation. One of the key factors to experiencing God's presence is to allow yourself to be present.

Let's return to the example in Chapter Five. We established that you are mentally and emotionally present in a situation where you think you are being manipulated. You have also acknowledged that you are feeling fear. You recognized the presence of God within your thoughts and feelings in the situation you are experiencing. Now, let's just say that you have noticed this is a pattern in your life, or that the Lord's presence didn't just resolve the issue. What can you do now? You can take inventory of your heart and find out why this is happening.

Allow yourself to stay in the presence of God. Then, right in your situation, in your thoughts and feelings, you can ask God questions.

While asking these questions, you can receive information from God in any way. It can be a thought, a picture, a feeling, or you can sense it, remember it, or even just know it. Pay attention to the very first impression you get. It may not make any sense to your understanding and it could be specific or abstract. You could also disagree with the information you get. We are addressing the head/heart disconnect, and it won't make sense all the time. It is important that you receive and pay attention to the first impression, however you get that information.

Ask God these questions:

1) Right there, where I think **I am being manipulated** and I feel **afraid,** what is the truth of my identity?

Remember, your heart may or may not let you receive this answer, depending on the lie you are believing and the self-protection you are using. When asking this question, you could get a true answer that you consider good or a lie that you consider to be bad. Sometimes the lie you believe is so strong that you will get that answer instead of the truth. Simple discernment: If it is not an answer that lines up with the truth of Jesus Christ and who He says you are in Scripture, it is a lie. If you did ask this question and you got an answer that is a lie, then you don't need to ask the second question. You already have that answer. For this example, let's say that you got an impression that was good and true. You heard, sensed, or thought that "You are strong." Now we can move on to the next question.

2) Right there where **I think I am being manipulated** and I feel **afraid,** what is the lie I am believing?

Again, allow yourself to pay attention to the very first impression you get. It doesn't have to make sense to you or the situation. Just allow yourself to get the information. For this example, let's say that you felt a sense of timidity – like you can't stand up for yourself. That sense can be translated into the lie that "I am timid and can't stand up for myself." Now we can move on to the next question.

3) What self-protection manifests because I believe that **I am timid and can't stand up for myself?**

Whatever happens, or whatever you become aware of after this question, is your self-protection. You may see something, remember something, feel something, or just start experiencing an emotion or behavior. Remember, you can get this information in any way. It is also possible that this system is so familiar to you, you don't even recognize that it is running. Again, if you have any trouble with this, I recommend getting help from someone. Let's say for this example that you got a sense of, and could almost see yourself pulling away and retreating from, the situation. That sense and image can be translated into your self-protection being **pulling away and retreating.** We are not challenging this system. It does what it needs to because of the lie that **I am timid and can't stand up for myself.** Now that we have that information, we can move on to the next question.

4) If I did not believe that **I am timid and can't stand up for myself,** and I didn't have to protect myself with **pulling away and retreating,** what would I have?

Pay attention to whatever you become aware of after the question. Again, this answer could be something you consider to be good or bad. There is no expectation of what it should be.

If the answer is something that you don't consider to be good and true – this would just be the next starting point for the same four questions. You would just start this process over from that place.

If the answer is something you consider to be good and true – we can move on to see what your heart wants to do about this information. For this example, let's say the answer was good. You got a sense of confidence and you could even feel yourself straighten up.

Here is all that information laid out as a grid:

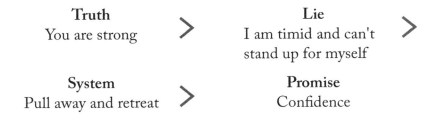

Truth		**Lie**	
You are strong	>	I am timid and can't stand up for myself	>

System		**Promise**
Pull away and retreat	>	Confidence

Remember, the truth of who you are is already true in Christ. You are strong and confident as a new creation. In this example, you are pulling away and retreating because you believe you are timid and can't stand up for yourself. This would be an example of how what you know and what you believe can be so starkly different. The problem is, we don't live out of what we know, we live out of what we believe. Denying what is actually happening and telling yourself how you should behave doesn't help you. It doesn't help you find out what is causing the behavior and it doesn't help you be free. Anywhere that you are not expressing the true nature of your identity in Christ, you absolutely can be free, no longer needing to self-protect.

"Anywhere that you are not expressing the true nature of your identity in Christ, you absolutely can be free, no longer needing to self-protect."

Now that you have stayed present, and have taken inventory, you can review that information and see what your heart wants to do about it. We will look at this in the next few chapters.

PRACTICAL APPLICATION

For this practical application we are going to follow up from where you finished with the Three Steps to Life.

Now that you have practiced the three steps and know how to stay present, choose reality, and connect with God, we can take inventory of your heart. We just went over the steps in a hypothetical situation. Now you can apply it to your life, personally.

You can start fresh or you can revisit one of the areas where you were feeling fear, shame, or guilt and have already been practicing. Either way, once you have connected with God in an area where you are not experiencing the kingdom, let's find out more information.

It can be a thought, a picture, a feeling, or you can sense it, remember it, or even just know it. Pay attention to the very first impression you get. It may not make any sense to your understanding, and it could be specific or abstract. You could also disagree with the information you get.

This is a process of allowing you to be present in your body and in your situation. Let yourself truly be present where you are.

We have already established that we are working on an area where you are not experiencing righteousness, peace, and joy, so let's take inventory there. Allow God to reveal truth to you, in whatever way He is bringing revelation. Remember, it doesn't have to be any particular way. Once you have allowed yourself to be present with your situation, your thoughts, your feelings, and with God – ask Him these questions:

1) *"Right there, where I think* _____ *and*

I feel _____, *what is the truth of my identity?"*

You can use this space for your answer:

_____

_____

_____

Remember, you don't have to "press in" and make yourself get an answer. Just pay attention to the first impression of what happens after the question. Your heart may or may not let you receive this answer, depending on the lie you are believing and the self-protection you are using. Also, you could get a true or untrue answer. Sometimes the lie you believe is so strong that you will get the lie instead of the truth. If you did ask this question and you got an answer that was untrue, then you don't need to ask the second question. You just answered it for yourself.

Now we can move on to the next question.

2) *"Right there, where I think* _____ *and*

I feel _____, *what is the lie I am believing?"*

You can use this space for your answer:

_____

_____

_____

Allow yourself to pay attention to the very first impression you get. It doesn't have to make sense to you or the situation. Just allow yourself to get the information.

Now we can move on to the next question.

3) *"What self-protection manifests because I believe the lie*_____

_____ *?"*

You can use this space for your answer:

_____

_____

_____

Whatever happens, or whatever you become aware of after this question, is your self-protection. You may see something, remember something, feel something, or just start experiencing an emotion or behavior. You can get this information in any way, and it doesn't have to make any sense. It is also possible that this system is so familiar to you, that you won't easily recognize it. Be very sensitive to everything while you are doing this.

Now we can move on to the next question.

4) *"If I did not believe* _____, *and I didn't*

have to protect myself with _____,

what would I have?"

You can use this space for your answer:

_____

_____

_____

Pay attention to whatever you become aware of after the question. Remember, this answer could be something you consider to be good and true, or something you consider to be bad and untrue. There is no expectation of what it should be.

Let yourself just stay in the presence of the Lord, and remember, this is just information. In the following chapters we will see what your heart wants to do about this information.

CHAPTER SEVEN

FORGIVENESS

Forgiveness is a key element to a lifestyle of freedom and healing. Without it, we end up living a life filled with turmoil, hurt, anger, and broken relationships. For some, forgiveness can be a very confusing thing. So often, someone I am coaching will tell me they have already forgiven a particular person, over and over again. The problem they are having is they still get triggered every time they see that person, and they have an unhealthy reaction to them. They will get angry, afraid, ashamed, or feel the emotional hurt, and then have to try and forgive them all over again. This cycle continues and they just can't seem to get over the past.

There are several potential reasons for this. It could even be a boundaries issue rather than a forgiveness issue. Meaning, they could be allowing certain behaviors from people without setting appropriate relational or physical boundaries. In this chapter, we will look at just the forgiveness issues.

One of the potential reasons for that forgiveness cycle could be that well-meaning people who are trying to forgive, unintentionally engage in a practice of self-righteous judgmentalism instead of forgiveness.

This is a different problem than simply not being able or willing to forgive. When dealing with the problem of self-righteous judgmentalism, you may think you have forgiven, but it seems like it didn't work.

Hopefully, this chapter will help you to be able to truly forgive and be free in areas where you are still stuck and hurting.

Let's start with looking at four of the Greek words used for forgiveness in the New Testament. Here they are with some corresponding Scriptures:

> Judge not, and you will not be judged; condemn not, and you will not be condemned; forgive, and you will be forgiven.
> – Luke 6:37

Forgive – the Greek word used here is *apolyō* (Strong's G630). It means: to free fully, relieve, release, dismiss, let die, pardon, divorce, let depart, forgive, let go, loose, send away, release, set at liberty.

> In Him we have redemption through His blood, the forgiveness of our trespasses, according to the riches of His grace. – Ephesians 1:7

Forgiveness – the Greek word used here is *aphesis* (Strong's G859). It means: freedom, pardon, deliverance, forgiveness, liberty, remission.

> And He said to them, when you pray, say: "Father, hallowed be Your name. Your kingdom come. Give us each day our

daily bread, and forgive us our sins, for we ourselves forgive everyone who is indebted to us. And lead us not into temptation." – Luke 11:2-4

Forgive – the Greek word used here is *aphiēmi* (Strong's G863). It means: to send forth, cry, forgive, forsake, lay aside, leave, let alone, let be, let go, let have, omit, send away, remit, suffer, yield up.

And you, who were dead in your trespasses and the uncircumcision of your flesh, God made alive together with Him, having forgiven us all our trespasses. – Colossians 2:13

Forgiven – the Greek word used here is *charizomai* (Strong's G5483). It means: to grant as a favor, gratuitously, in kindness, pardon or rescue, deliver, forgive, freely give, grant.

To help us understand what God is saying when He talks about forgiveness, here is a list of the different expressions of all four of those Greek words:

cry	lay aside	release
deliver	leave	relieve
dismiss	let alone	remission
divorce	let be	remit
forgive	let depart	rescue
forgiveness	let die	send away
forsake	let go	set at liberty
freedom	let have	suffer
freely give	liberty	to free fully
grant	loose	to grant as a favor
gratuitously	omit	to send forth
in kindness	pardon	yield up

Now that we have looked at the expanded meaning of those words, let's look at a few specific Scriptures that have really helped form my understanding of forgiveness and have helped many people receive freedom.

> Be kind to one another, tenderhearted, forgiving (G5483) one another, as God in Christ forgave you. – Ephesians 4:32

> Put on then, as God's chosen ones, holy and beloved, compassionate hearts, kindness, humility, meekness, and patience, bearing with one another and, if one has a complaint against another, forgiving (G5483) each other; as the Lord has forgiven you, so you also must forgive. – Colossians 3:12-13

These two Scriptures seem to express that we forgive "as" the Lord forgave us. This is different than forgiving "because" the Lord forgave us. He covers that concept in other Scriptures.

As – the Greek word used here is *kathōs* (Strong's G2531). It means: just as, in as much as, according to, even as, how.

An expression of the Scripture including the fullness of this definition could be:

> *As God's chosen ones, holy and beloved, put on compassionate hearts, kindness, humility, meekness, and patience. Bear with one another, and be kind and tenderhearted to one another. If one has a complaint against another, forgive one another, just as, in as much as, according to, even as, and how God in Christ forgave you, so you also must forgive.*

With that definition and expression in mind, let's look at those Scriptures again. They seem to be expressing that we forgive in the same way, just as, according to, and how Jesus forgave us. So the question is, how were we forgiven? Again, my *Who Do You Think You Are?* Bible study workbook[1] answers that question in depth. If you haven't had the chance to work through that yet, here are a few Scriptures to review:

> In Him we have redemption through His blood, the forgiveness (G859) of our trespasses, according to the riches of His grace. – Ephesians 1:7

> Now as they were eating, Jesus took bread, and after blessing it broke it and gave it to the disciples, and said, "Take, eat; this is My body." And He took a cup, and when He had given thanks He gave it to them, saying, "Drink of it, all of you, for this is My blood of the covenant, which is poured out for many for the forgiveness (G859) of sins. – Matthew 26:26-28

The redemption and forgiveness we have is through the blood of Jesus, that was poured out on the cross, according to the riches of His grace. Jesus being crucified is how we were forgiven. We forgive by the blood of Jesus Christ.

"The redemption and forgiveness we have is through the blood of Jesus, that was poured out on the cross, according to the riches of His grace."

Let's look at the difference between forgiveness and self-righteous judgmentalism.

Forgiveness does not require us to understand what has happened to those who have hurt us so we can try to stir up compassion. We don't need to know how they were hurt, or why they did what they did. Understanding is not part of the forgiveness process. Trying to use understanding to stir up compassion, so we can forgive, is part of the reason it seems like forgiveness doesn't always work.

I have seen this process of trying to understand lead to thinking similar to: "They did the best they could" or "They had a really rough life." These are just two examples. There are many variations of this theme. In these examples, there is a sense of trying to understand and have compassion for the person who may have hurt us, so we can forgive them. We believe that having compassion and understanding will make it easier to forgive. Yes, I know that sounds good, but let's explore what that really is.

"Trying to use understanding to stir up compassion, so that we can forgive, is part of the reason it seems like forgiveness doesn't always work."

If you look at what that process really is, you will see what is happening is not forgiveness at all. We can call it whatever we want, but trying to analyze the life of someone who hurt you, so you can stir up compassion in order to forgive them, isn't compassion. It doesn't work because that is just us looking at what happened to them and then judging whether it was bad enough, according to our self-defined standards, to give them the right to be forgiven. That is us deciding whether they deserve to be forgiven or not, and determining whether their pain and suffering was bad enough to warrant forgiveness. That is not compassion or forgiveness; that is self-righteous judgmentalism. This is one of the possible reasons why, even though you think you may have forgiven someone one hundred times, you still get triggered and have an unhealthy reaction every time you see them. It may be because you have not forgiven them, you have just self-righteously judged them one hundred times. That may be why forgiveness "hasn't worked."

Another aspect I hear is something like: "I've done the same thing; how can I hold that against them?" This may sound good as well. Yet this is just us basing forgiveness off of our own behavior instead of the blood of Jesus Christ. Think about that for a minute. How ridiculous is that? Again, this is self-righteous judgmentalism and not forgiveness.

---

*"The completeness of the blood of
Jesus brings freedom and healing."*

One of the additional problems with both of these examples is it requires some sort of intellectual filing system to manage all this information. Somehow we have to keep track of all of our behaviors, other people's behaviors, and those self-defined standards of forgiveness. That is a lot of work, and it does not bring freedom and healing. The completeness of the blood of Jesus brings freedom and healing.

> And you, who were dead in your trespasses and the uncircumcision of your flesh, God made alive together with Him, having forgiven (G5483) us all our trespasses, by canceling the record of debt that stood against us with its legal demands. This He set aside, nailing it to the cross.
> – Colossians 2:13-14

Thank You, Jesus!

> *"If we have been crucified with Christ to the world, the world has been crucified to us, and it is no longer we who live but it is Christ who lives in us, then who owes us anything?"*

The other aspect of forgiveness I want to look at is when we won't forgive, or think we are unable to forgive. Jesus allowed Himself to be crucified on the cross to cancel the debt for our sins. For some reason though, we tend to have some debts that we cannot or will not release. If we look at the first two Scriptures we started with, remember the Lord is asking us to forgive as He forgave. I think one of the aspects of forgiving is us allowing our old selves to be crucified with Christ to release the debts we believe people owe us. Now, let's be clear, I am not suggesting that we should be other people's saviors. What I am suggesting is that we truly believe the good news and allow our old self to be crucified with Christ.

> I have been crucified with Christ. It is no longer I who live, but Christ who lives in me. And the life I now live in the flesh I live by faith in the Son of God, who loved me and gave Himself for me. – Galatians 2:20

> But far be it from me to boast except in the cross of our Lord Jesus Christ, by which the world has been crucified to me, and I to the world. – Galatians 6:14

By faith, we have been crucified with Christ. It is no longer we who live. It is Christ living in us. We have been fully crucified to the world. The world has been fully crucified to us. We are no longer that old self, and we no longer need to hold on to those old dead debts of the world.

If we have been crucified with Christ to the world, the world has been crucified to us, and it is no longer we who live but it is Christ who lives in us, then who owes us anything?

---

*"The truth is, it is absolutely possible
to forgive everybody for everything
that we are still holding on to."*

Our inability or unwillingness to forgive is based on a lie. There are many variations of lies the enemy uses to poison us with unforgiveness. Yes, we may have been wounded; I am not discounting the experiences and the emotional hurt. However, these lies are just a rejection of the work of Jesus Christ on the cross. Sometimes we don't even know what those lies are, or we don't want to accept that they are lies.

The truth is, it is absolutely possible to forgive everybody for everything that we are still holding on to. Forgiveness and freedom are available in Christ.

With this truth in mind, I have one more Scripture that has helped form my beliefs about forgiveness.

Anyone whom you forgive, I also forgive. Indeed, what I have forgiven (G5483), if I have forgiven anything, has been for your sake in the presence of Christ, so that we would not be outwitted by Satan; for we are not ignorant of his designs. – 2 Corinthians 2:10-11

This Scripture has inspired me to apply the concepts from the "Three Steps to Life" into my practice of forgiveness. What I mean is that

I intentionally allow myself to be aware of the presence of Jesus whenever I am forgiving someone. Applying this process helps me to find out if there is a lie that is in the way of forgiveness.

Forgive in the presence of Christ, through the blood of Jesus, by the power of the Holy Spirit, allowing the old self to be crucified, thereby canceling any debt owed to you. This will transform your life. Incorporating these principles into your life will allow you to easily forgive and be set free from the burden of unforgiveness.

> For freedom Christ has set us free; stand firm therefore, and do not submit again to a yoke of slavery. – Galatians 5:1

PRACTICAL APPLICATION

Now that we have looked at the principles of forgiveness, we can apply them to any areas where we have intentionally not forgiven, or where we have self-righteously judged instead of forgiven. We will have the opportunity to release any of the unforgiveness, hurt, self-righteous judgments, and filing systems we have been using.

I will give you an overview of the process and then walk you through it. You can engage with this as much as your heart is ready. Your heart doesn't have to do anything it doesn't want to do. It may still not be ready to forgive. If that is the case, I would recommend having patience for yourself and seeking trusted help.

This is what we are going to do: We are going to allow ourselves to be in the presence of God, acknowledge any unforgiveness, repent from the self-righteous judgmentalism, release all the false standards and any filing systems, forgive, and then receive truth.

If you are ready, let's go:

Let yourself think about any area of hurt or unforgiveness that you are aware of. Then, right there in that area of hurt or unforgiveness, apply the "Three Steps to Life" and allow yourself to be present in the presence of God.

I recommend that you express the forgiveness out loud, during this process. I believe that the spoken word is powerful.

> Since we have the same spirit of faith according to what has been written, "I believed, and so I spoke," we also believe, and so we also speak. – 2 Corinthians 4:13

Once you have acknowledged the presence of God, you can apply the truth of Galatians 6:14 in that area of your heart. You can do this by asking Jesus to establish the truth of the cross, what He accomplished on the cross, right there in your heart between you and any person you are forgiving. This truth is already true. In reality, you are only asking Him to help you acknowledge that truth. He could represent this to you in any way. You could see it, feel it, know it, sense it, or have it established any way that makes sense to your heart. It is also a good practice to ask Holy Spirit to help at this point in the process.

Ask Jesus: *"Jesus, would You please establish the truth of the cross, and what You accomplished on the cross, between me, and* (whoever you are forgiving)*?"*

Allow Jesus to establish this in whatever way your heart can receive it. Invite the Holy Spirit in, however it is comfortable for you.

Now that you have acknowledged God's presence and the truth of the cross right there in your heart, let's repent from any self-righteous judgmentalism.

Ask God: *"Are there any false standards of forgiveness I have established?"*

As the Lord reveals, let's repent.

"Jesus, I am sorry for any false standards and self-righteous judgmentalism that I used instead of forgiving."

"I break agreement with all the false standards, all the self-righteousness, and all the judgmentalism I used."

"I release to You all of that information, all the ways I kept track of that information, and all the ways I gathered that information."

"Holy Spirit, would you please remove all of that information?"

Allow God to remove all of that. You can experience this in any way. You may feel lighter, you may see Him doing something, you may get impressions of people or events. Just stay with Jesus and the Holy Spirit.

Before moving on, let's ask the Holy Spirit a question.

"Holy Spirit, is there anything You would like to give me in return?"

Again, just let yourself receive.

You can use this space for your answer:

_____

_____

_____

Now, let's forgive.

"Jesus, I come into agreement with You and Your forgiveness, and I completely forgive (whoever you are forgiving) *by Your blood, through the power of the Holy Spirit."*

"I release them completely, and agree that they owe me nothing."

Now, let yourself breathe. Enjoy the freedom of forgiveness.

Follow the lead of the Holy Spirit, and forgive and release as much as you need to.

When you are finished, you can thank Jesus any way you feel led, and then we can ask Him one last question.

Ask Jesus: *"Is there anything else You want me to know?"*

You can use this space for your answer:

_____

_____

_____

Endnotes:

1.   faithbygrace.org/resources

CHAPTER EIGHT

REPENT AND BELIEVE

So far we have intentionally stayed present, chosen reality, and connected with God. We have acknowledged the presence of God in our thoughts and our feelings, right in the situation we are in. We have taken inventory of our hearts. We found out the truth of who we are, any lies we believe, and the self-protections we are using. We found out what we would have if we didn't believe the lies and didn't have to self-protect. We have also forgiven anybody connected to the lies that needed to be released. Now it is time to repent from any lies and receive the truth.

> The time is fulfilled, and the kingdom of God is at hand;
> repent and believe in the gospel. – Mark 1:15

The ability to apply the kingdom principle of repentance will drastically transform your life.

Let's look at the definition of "repent" and then examine the Scripture in light of this definition.

Repent – the Greek word used here is *metanoeō* (Strong's G3340). It means: to think differently, reconsider – repent.

An expression of the Scripture including the fullness of that definition could be:

> *The time is fulfilled, and the kingdom of God is at hand; reconsider your thoughts, repent, think differently, and believe in the gospel.*

The Lord is calling us to change our thinking. Think about that. Repentance is about thinking, not behavior. This is why, in Chapter Five, I recommended that we choose reality in the "Three Steps to Life" and actually think our thoughts. You cannot reconsider a thought you are having, repent from it, and think differently, if you won't acknowledge what you are thinking. This is why repentance has to be part of a practical and sustainable lifestyle of freedom and healing.

> *"You cannot reconsider a thought you are having, repent from it, and think differently, if you won't acknowledge what you are thinking."*

In Mark 1:15, the Lord is telling us to reconsider the lies we believe, think differently, and believe the good news. Changing our thinking is starkly different than changing our behavior. Focusing on and trying to change our behavior, instead of focusing on the thoughts that are manifesting that behavior, is not repentance and will not help us live a lifestyle of freedom.

> We destroy arguments and every lofty opinion raised against the knowledge of God, and take every thought captive to obey Christ. – 2 Corinthians 10:5

"Denying our thoughts and behaving in a way that appears righteous is not peaceful, is not joyful, and is not the kingdom of God."

So often I discover that people are operating in denial and calling it faith. Denying our thoughts and behaving in a way that appears righteous is not peaceful, is not joyful, and is not the kingdom of God. Remember, the kingdom of God is righteousness, peace, and joy in the Holy Spirit.

> Jesus answered them, "This is the work of God, that you believe in Him whom He has sent." – John 6:29

Let's look at the definition of "believe" and then examine the Scripture in light of this definition.

Believe – the Greek word used here is *pisteuō* (Strong's G4100). It means: to have faith in, to entrust, believe, commit to trust, put in trust with.

An expression of the Scripture including the fullness of that definition could be:

> *This is the work of God, that you have faith in, entrust, commit to trust in, and believe in Him whom He has sent.*

This word believe (G4100) is the same word used in Mark 1:15.

An expression of these two Scriptures together could be:

The time is fulfilled, and the kingdom of God is at hand. This is the work of God, that you reconsider your thoughts, repent, and think differently. Have faith in, commit to trust in, and believe the gospel of Him whom He has sent.

One of my favorite Scriptures that expresses the concept of repentance is in the book of Isaiah.

For thus said the Lord GOD, the Holy One of Israel, "In repentance and rest you shall be saved; in quietness and in trust shall be your strength." – Isaiah 30:15

This Scripture from Isaiah is a beautiful expression of what God is saying in Mark 1:15. It is essentially saying the exact same thing. Reconsidering the thoughts we are having, repenting, and thinking differently will bring healing. Having faith in, trusting, and believing in Jesus will bring strength. If you can't find righteousness, peace, and joy in your thought life, you won't find it anywhere else in your life. Applying the aspects of repentance to your thought life will bring healing and strength to your whole life.

"If you can't find righteousness, peace, and joy in your thought life, you won't find it anywhere else in your life."

A few more examples of the blessing and power of repentance are:

Repent therefore, and turn back, that your sins may be blotted out, that times of refreshing may come from the presence of the Lord, and that He may send the Christi appointed for you, Jesus. – Acts 3:19-20

When they heard these things they fell silent. And they glorified God, saying, "Then to the Gentiles also God has granted repentance that leads to life." – Acts 11:18

For godly grief produces a repentance that leads to salvation without regret, whereas worldly grief produces death. – 2 Corinthians 7:10

Repentance leads to life and salvation without regret, and brings times of refreshing from the presence of the Lord. Repentance does not bring condemnation, punishment, humiliation, shame, regret, or death. You do not have to make yourself feel bad to feel better. There is no condemnation in Christ (Romans 8:1). Condemnation is the tangible evidence of lack of faith, and the actual proof that you are believing a lie. That would be a good test to see if you are truly repenting or if you are doing something else. Repentance leads to life.

"You do not have to make yourself feel bad to feel better."

In 2 Corinthians 13:5, the Word tells us to examine ourselves and see if we are in the faith, to test ourselves and see if we realize that Jesus Christ is in us. Anywhere in our hearts that we are experiencing fear, shame, or guilt, in any of its various forms, we are unaware that Jesus Christ is in us. This is one of the key Scriptures for the understanding of our need for inner healing. If we are not in faith, we need to examine ourselves and find out what we are in. Then we can reconsider the arguments and every lofty opinion we have raised against the knowledge of God, take those thoughts captive, and change our thinking to believe the gospel, in obedience to Christ.

That is repentance, and it will bring life.

PRACTICAL APPLICATION

For this practical application, we are going to look at the definitions of some of the words in 2 Corinthians 10:5, and then examine the Scripture in light of these definitions.

> We destroy arguments and every lofty opinion raised against the knowledge of God, and take every thought captive to obey Christ. – 2 Corinthians 10:5

Destroy – the Greek word used here is *kathaireō* (Strong's G2507). It means: to lower, demolish, cast down, pull down, put down, take down, destroy.

Arguments – the Greek word used here is *logismos* (Strong's G3053). It means: computation, reasoning, imagination, thought.

Lofty opinion – the Greek word used here is *hypsōma* (Strong's G5313). It means: an elevated place or thing, altitude, a barrier, height, high thing.

Raised – the Greek word used here is *epairō* (Strong's G1869). It means: to raise up, exalt self, poise, lift up, take up.

Thought – the Greek word used here is *noēma* (Strong's G163). It means: a perception, purpose, the intellect, disposition, device, mind, thought.

Obey – the Greek word used here is *hypakoē* (Strong's G5218). It means: attentive hearkening, compliance, submission, obedience, make obedient, obey.

An expression of the Scripture including the fullness of those definitions could be:

> *We lower, demolish, cast down, pull down, put down, take down, and destroy computations, reasonings, imaginations, thoughts, or arguments, and every elevated place, altitude, barrier, height, high thing, or lofty opinion raised up, exalted, or poised against the knowledge of God, and take every perception, purpose, intellect, disposition, device, mind, and thought captive to attentively hearken, be compliant to, submit to, and obey Christ.*

Now, let's take a moment to ask God some questions. As you do this, let yourself freely receive the first impression and fill in the blanks with the answers you get.

Ask God: *"What computations, reasonings, imaginations, thoughts, or arguments have I raised up, exalted, or poised against the knowledge of You?"*

_____

_____

_____

_____

Ask God: *"What elevated place, altitude, barrier, height, high thing or lofty opinion have I raised up, exalted, or poised against the knowledge of You?"*

_____

_____

_____

_____

Ask God: *"How do You want me to lower, demolish, cast down, pull down, put down, take down, and destroy those?"*

_____

_____

_____

_____

Ask God: *"What perceptions, purposes, intellects, dispositions, devices, mindsets, and thoughts do I need to capture?"*

_____

_____

Ask God: *"Now that I have captured those, how do I bring them into obedience, compliance, and submission to Christ?"*

Ask God: *"With what truth do You want me to replace those captured perceptions, purposes, intellects, dispositions, devices, mindsets, and thoughts?"*

Ask God: *"What Scriptures would help me to rise above these arguments, lofty opinions, and thoughts?"*

_____

_____

_____

_____

Now that you have all this information, you can reconsider these arguments, lofty opinions, and thoughts. You can think differently, repent, submit your thoughts in obedience to Christ, and believe in the gospel.

If you are ready, here is an example of how you can do that:

"Lord, I am so sorry that I raised up arguments, opinions, imaginations, and reasonings against the knowledge of God. In Jesus' name, I break all agreement, take down, destroy, and renounce _____ (fill in all of your arguments, opinions, imaginations, reasonings, elevated places, altitudes, barriers, heights, high things or lofty opinions He revealed to you).*"*

"I repent from _____ (list every perception, purpose, intellect, disposition, device, mind, and thought He revealed to you).*"*

"I come into agreement with the truth _____ (fill in the truth and the Scriptures He revealed to you), *and submit all my thoughts to obedience in Christ."*

"Thank You, Jesus."

CHAPTER NINE

DEMONS AND DETAILS

In this chapter we are going to briefly look at two subjects: demons and details. Over the 15 years of ministering to people's hearts, we have learned a lot. We have noticed certain patterns of behaviors, recognized helpful and unhelpful approaches to issues, and become aware of some of the enemy's strategies for destruction. One of those strategies is to keep all of us focused on the details of the events of our past to keep us continually battling the demons in those details. Let's look at the details first.

DETAILS

You may already understand this next concept I am going to share. However, for some, it may be a pretty dramatic shift. I want to first make it clear that God absolutely cares about what happened to you. All of us have had traumatic experiences that have affected us. This is not in any way an attempt to discount what happened to you, or minimize the pain and hurt you have experienced. With that in mind, prayerfully consider this: The details of the events of your life, even the most traumatic ones, are ineffective to the process of healing, reconciliation, and freedom.

"The details of the events of your life, even the most traumatic ones, are ineffective to the process of healing, reconciliation, and freedom."

Confession is a key principle in repentance, and there is a time that is appropriate for you to express and confess something that you may have never talked about. This is different than what we are going to look at. Here is a proverb that expresses what I am talking about:

Like a dog that returns to his vomit is a fool who repeats his folly. – Proverbs 26:11

Many people have taken the details of the traumatic events of their life and translated them into stories they regurgitate in their minds and in their conversations, over and over again. They will play back the details of the events, then eat them all back up, go to another conversation, and then regurgitate the details on someone else. This is foolish according to the Scriptures. This pattern is not beneficial for your life and does not bring freedom. You will see this foolishness in conversations such as a play by play of, "They said, I said, they said, I said!" This pattern may also come into play in conversations when two people debate the details of what they said or did, trying to defend themselves, instead of engaging in a process of reconciliation.

We have found that in these situations, the only information that is helpful in the healing and reconciliation process is the truth, what we actually believe, how we are self-protecting, and what we would have if we didn't believe a lie and self-protect in that situation. That is the information that will help us to be able to repent, believe the gospel, and experience righteousness, peace, and joy.

If you find yourself reviewing and replaying old traumatic events in your mind or in your conversations, that is an indicator that you may be believing and living out of lies, instead of believing and living out of truth. That pattern will keep you from being able to be present, experience life, and enjoy the good things you have.

> Therefore, confess your sins to one another and pray for one another, that you may be healed. The prayer of a righteous person has great power as it is working. – James 5:16

If we live a lifestyle where we actually get to the root sin, confess it, and pray, we will be healed. Unfortunately, we so often see people stuck in a loop of confessing the fruit, and expressing the self-protections of the root lie, continually reviewing the pain and hurt, and never getting healed. The root lie is the real sin. If we can confess the root lie, repent, and believe the truth, we will be healed. There are many times when we have no idea what that root lie is. That is why we need help from others. Unfortunately, some will continually review the details of their past with themselves and others, without ever getting any real help.

"As you get free of the lies, you will get free of the hurt and pain."

Two different people could have two completely different traumatic events, with no similar details, and end up believing the same exact lie. That is why the details are not the important part of the process. Focusing on the details will keep you experiencing the emotional hurt and pain from the lies that are connected to the traumatic events. The lies are the cause of the hurt and pain you are experiencing. As you get free of the lies, you will get free of the hurt and pain. Then you will find that you won't need to review or replay the details in your mind or in your conversations. You may even begin to forget some of the details that were causing you pain and had you stuck in a loop.

The pattern the Lord has consistently demonstrated for us in His Word has been a remembrance and celebration of the victories and good things in life. Whether it was a tradition, custom, feast, festival, or memorial stones of remembrance being established, it doesn't seem to be His intention that we focus on and remember the bad things that have happened.

> Remember not the former things, nor consider the things of old. Behold, I am doing a new thing; now it springs forth, do you not perceive it? – Isaiah 43:18-19

> Brothers, I do not consider that I have made it my own. But one thing I do: forgetting what lies behind and straining forward to what lies ahead, I press on toward the goal for the prize of the upward call of God in Christ Jesus. – Philippians 3:13-14

"Repenting, believing the truth, and no longer focusing on the lies and details of your past will manifest freedom, peace, and the fruit of the Spirit."

There is a difference between forgetting and denial. Denial will still manifest the hurt, pain, and fruit from the lies of your past. Repenting, believing the truth, and no longer focusing on the lies and details of your past will manifest freedom, peace, and the fruit of the Spirit. This will help you live in the present and press on toward your future. You will know the difference by the fruit. One brings fear, shame, and guilt. The other brings righteousness, peace, and joy.

DEMONS

In my journey of helping others walk through healing, I have worked with people who have some of the most horrific stories you can imagine. They have stories of abuse, trauma, broken relationships, and demonic oppression. As I have already pointed out, there is no need to get lost in the details while pursuing healing. Not only will it be easier for you to personally process, it is also a good layer of protection for any caregiver that may be helping you.

Now let's focus on the demonic oppression. In all the people we have worked with, it has been very rare that there was a demonic issue we needed to take care of. Only about one out of every twenty people who have come to us over the years were claiming demonic oppression. Out of that small group of people, only about one out of every ten of them actually had a demonic issue we had to deal with directly. Most of the time when people come in thinking they are experiencing demonic oppression, we find that it is actually just their own systems of self-protection that are running. Out of the thousands and thousands of people we have individually ministered to through the years, we have only had a handful of demonic manifestations.

As believers, in Jesus' name we have the authority to cast out demons if necessary (Mark 16:17). It is something that needs to be addressed sometimes. Although I have found if we cast out a demon and the person we are working with is still in agreement with it, that can be a problem. Personally, I don't think we need to give the demonic as much attention and credit as some people do. When I am working with someone, I will help them find the lie (demonic agreement), allow them to repent, and then ask the Holy Spirit to remove any demonic influence. It is a very simple process that works. For this book, we are just focusing on personal freedom and healing. We are not going to delve into teaching on the demonic realm. For more information on that subject and how to be free, I recommend Faith Blatchford's book *Winning The Battle For The Night*[1].

Even if it is a demonic issue we are dealing with, the real problem is still the lies we are believing. Without an agreement with the lie, the enemy has no authority in our lives. The easiest way I have found to do demonic deliverance is to invite Jesus into the situation. After your heart is aware of the presence of God, that issue is usually resolved. A demon usually only sticks around if it is allowed to because of a false agreement. Several times in healing and coaching sessions, I have even seen and experienced the demonic fleeing just before we discover the root lie. It is almost like they know they are about to lose their grip, so they leave on their own without any intervention. The lie itself is the demonic agreement. If you have broken agreement with the lie, you have broken the demonic agreement.

> Submit yourselves therefore to God. Resist the devil, and he will flee from you. – James 4:7

One of the ways that I have found it goes wrong is when certain behaviors or manifestations are deemed demonic without verification. Unfortunately, many of the people we have worked with have even needed healing from the demonic deliverance they have already received. That is why the intentional process of acknowledging the presence of God, and confirming what is really happening, is so important. Not having an agenda and not pre-determining what the problem is, before we pursue healing or help someone else, is essential. Having an agenda and thinking we have all the answers is dishonoring and potentially damaging.

One of the people I had the privilege of working with was brought to me because of an extreme demonic oppression. It was not just a system of self-protection. They were dealing with physical manifestations in their home and actual destruction of property. These manifestations would even follow them when they traveled. Even though they were dealing with that level of demonic attack, there were no manifestations in the session we had together. We identified the lies they believed, the self-protections they were using, and connected them to Jesus, Holy Spirit, and Father God. Once they were able to repent, forgive, and believe the truth, the demonic issue was resolved. We didn't even once have to confront the demonic directly. It is so much cleaner and easier that way.

> *"If we can live a life where we are not looking for demons, and we are not focusing on the details of the events of our past, we will find truth, peace, power, and the presence of God."*

Sadly, there are many people in battle mode, trying to find and take on all the demonic influences in their life. I have even had the honor of working with people who are gifted in seeing in the spirit and have been tricked into a lifestyle of demonic battle. These were people who would spend most of their time in the demonic and angelic realm battling with demons and dealing with darkness. Again, we were able to get them to a place of repentance, forgiveness, and faith without any direct confrontation or manifestations of the demonic. They are now able to be present, have healthy connection and relationships with other people, and live in peace. They live much happier lives now, no longer focusing on darkness and what the enemy is doing. They can now focus on the good things in life, and what the Lord is doing.

If we can live a life where we are not looking for demons, and we are not focusing on the details of the events in our past, we will find truth, peace, power, and the presence of God. We are confident in dealing with lies and demons if they manifest, although we are not looking for them.

The old idiom "the devil is in the details" comes to mind as I think about this. If you live in the details of your past, you will continually find the enemy and experience an unsettled lifestyle. Living in righteousness, peace, and joy is a much better pursuit.

> Whoever pursues righteousness and kindness will find life, righteousness, and honor. – Proverbs 21:21

PRACTICAL APPLICATION

In this practical application, let's establish some memorial stones of victory to replace any misery stones of defeat.

Here are some of the references to memorial stones, feasts, and remembrances in the Scriptures:

> So early in the morning Jacob took the stone that he had put under his head and set it up for a pillar and poured oil on the top of it. He called the name of that place Bethel, but the name of the city was Luz at the first. Then Jacob made a vow, saying, "If God will be with me and will keep me in this way that I go, and will give me bread to eat and clothing to wear, so that I come again to my father's house

in peace, then the LORD shall be my God, and this stone, which I have set up for a pillar, shall be God's house. And of all that you give me I will give a full tenth to you."
– Genesis 28:18-22

That this may be a sign among you. When your children ask in time to come, 'What do those stones mean to you?' then you shall tell them that the waters of the Jordan were cut off before the ark of the covenant of the LORD. When it passed over the Jordan, the waters of the Jordan were cut off. So these stones shall be to the people of Israel a memorial forever. – Joshua 4:6-7

Then Moses said to the people, "Remember this day in which you came out from Egypt, out of the house of slavery, for by a strong hand the LORD brought you out from this place. No leavened bread shall be eaten." – Exodus 13:3

Remember the Sabbath day, to keep it holy. Six days you shall labor, and do all your work, but the seventh day is a Sabbath to the LORD your God. On it you shall not do any work, you, or your son, or your daughter, your male servant, or your female servant, or your livestock, or the sojourner who is within your gates. For in six days the LORD made heaven and earth, the sea, and all that is in them, and rested on the seventh day. Therefore the LORD blessed the Sabbath day and made it holy. – Exodus 20:8-11

For behold, I create new heavens and a new earth, and the former things shall not be remembered or come into mind. But be glad and rejoice forever in that which I create; for behold, I create Jerusalem to be a joy, and her people to be a gladness. – Isaiah 65:17-18

For I received from the Lord what I also delivered to you, that the Lord Jesus on the night when He was betrayed took bread, and when He had given thanks, He broke it, and said, "This is My body, which is for you. Do this in remembrance of Me." In the same way also He took the cup, after supper, saying, "This cup is the new covenant in My blood. Do this, as often as you drink it, in remembrance of Me." For as often as you eat this bread and drink the cup, you proclaim the Lord's death until He comes.
– 1 Corinthians 11:23-26

Remember that you were at that time separated from Christ, alienated from the commonwealth of Israel and strangers to the covenants of promise, having no hope and without God in the world. But now in Christ Jesus you who once were far off have been brought near by the blood of Christ.
– Ephesians 2:12-13

Now let's establish your own memorial or remembrance.

Take a moment, with the Lord, and look back at your life and review the key moments when you have received freedom or you were delivered from a situation. If this is not something you are aware of, just ask the Lord where He would like to establish a memorial stone in your past. This can just be a fun, easy exercise.

The first step would be to implement the "Three Steps to Life" right there where the Lord wants to establish a memorial stone.

Ask God: *"What are the things that are true, honorable, just, pure, lovely, commendable, excellent, or worthy of praise, from this event that*

You want me to remember and think about?"

_____

_____

_____

_____

Ask God: *"How can I celebrate and remember these?"*

_____

_____

_____

_____

Ask God: *"What are some practical steps I can take to experience these truths and celebrate them in my life?"*

_____

_____

_____

_____

Now ask the Holy Spirit to empower you and make these truths more real in your life.

To finish off this time of remembrance, I recommend having a time of communion to celebrate and remember the body and the blood of Jesus.

Endnotes:

1.   faithblatchford.com

CHAPTER TEN

WHY PURSUE HEALING?

Jesus was sent to bind up the brokenhearted. In John 17:4 He tells us that He accomplished the work He was given to do. Remember, in Chapter Three we learned from the book of Ezekiel that Jesus removed our hearts of stone and gave us new hearts. He bound up and removed our broken hearts of stone and gave us new, pure hearts of flesh. Our hearts are whole. We are not broken.

> The Spirit of the Lord GOD is upon me, because the LORD has anointed me to bring good news to the poor; He has sent me to bind up the brokenhearted, to proclaim liberty to the captives, and the opening of the prison to those who are bound. – Isaiah 61:1

The only brokenness is in our thoughts, our imaginations, and our beliefs. These broken beliefs will then manifest behavior that does not align with the truth. What we know in our heads is sometimes different than what we believe in our hearts. This causes a frustrating and confusing cycle of disconnection in our lives between what we know, and how we behave. The enemy will try to get us to identify ourselves with these lies and behaviors. They are not our identity – we are pure, whole, and righteous in Christ.

I have found that everyone lives from what they believe in their heart. Some people live intentionally from their heart, and some live unintentionally from their heart. Regardless of how well we think we are managing life from our heads, we are actually living from our hearts. That is why it is pointless to try to hide, ignore, and deny anything troublesome that is going on in our hearts, and pretend like it isn't happening.

Denial and performance are very common in the different cultures and movements of the church. From conservative to charismatic communities, the performances may look different from one another, but the denial is the same. It is a subtle deception that promotes fear, shame, and guilt internally, while performing a behavioral expectation of the culture externally. It is never helpful in the pursuit of the kingdom of God, and it is not His righteousness.

> You blind Pharisee! First clean the inside of the cup and the plate, that the outside also may be clean. – Matthew 23:26

Matthew 23:26 is a demonstration of what denial and performance look like. Not addressing the lies and wounds that are in our hearts and attempting to follow rules and perform to the cultural expectations is just like cleaning the outside of a dirty cup. The Word describes that behavior as pharisaical blindness. Those lies and wounds will manifest in our lives no matter how hard we pretend and try to keep the outside of the cup looking clean.

One of the first steps in living a lifestyle of freedom is to be honest with yourself. There is no freedom in denial, because you can't get freedom from something you don't have. Remember, we are not creating any new truth. The truth of who we are in Christ is already true. We are just choosing to intentionally pursue that truth and glorify God. If we don't look and behave exactly like Jesus, it is because we are believing lies and self-protecting. Pursuing inner healing through finding out what lies we believe and what self-protections we are using, repenting of those, and believing the truth, is not some sort of dangerous heresy; it is obedience to the Word of God.

Turn away from evil and do good; seek peace and pursue it. – Psalm 34:14

"Living an internal lifestyle of fear, shame, and guilt while trying to live an external lifestyle of righteousness, peace, and joy is not faith."

Seeking peace is not just a nice idea. Inner healing is not just for the really wounded. Throughout Scripture it is expressed as a way of life in Christ. As we have already learned in 2 Corinthians 13:5, we are called to examine ourselves and see if we are in the faith. In James 5:16, the Word tells us to confess our sins to one another, and pray for one another, so we may be healed. Living an internal lifestyle of fear, shame, and guilt while trying to live an external lifestyle of righteousness, peace, and joy is not faith.

SANCTIFIED

As we have previously established, the truth of who we are is already true. This truth, and our sanctification in Christ, are very misunderstood concepts. Years ago, when I first started trying to understand what was being referred to as the sanctification "process," I

*"Our sanctification in Christ never
actually changes. The only thing that
does change is our beliefs about it."*

had trouble getting concise answers to my questions. The explanations
I would get seemed very unclear and inconsistent to me, so I started
researching it for myself. To my surprise, as I looked to the Scriptures,
I could not find a sanctification "process." What I found is that we are
sanctified in Christ. That truth is already true; it is not becoming true
through a process. From my understanding, the aspect of sanctification
that is a process would be the process of us repenting from the lies and
choosing to believe the truth of our sanctification. Our sanctification
in Christ never actually changes. The only thing that does change is
our beliefs about it. A fuller breakdown of our sanctification, according
to the Scriptures, can be found in Session One of my *Who Do You
Think You Are?* Bible study.[1]

Here are some Scriptures that describe our sanctification:

John 17:17 – We are sanctified: in truth, His Word is truth

John 17:19 – We are sanctified: in truth by the consecration
of Jesus Christ

Acts 26:18 – We are sanctified: by faith

Romans 15:16 – We are sanctified: by the Holy Spirit

1 Corinthians 1:2 – We are sanctified: in Christ Jesus

1 Corinthians 6:11 – We were sanctified: in the name of the
Lord Jesus Christ by the Spirit of our God

Ephesians 5:26 – We are sanctified: by the washing of water with the Word

1 Thessalonians 5:23 – We are sanctified: "completely" by the God of peace Himself

2 Thessalonians 2:13 – We are sanctified: by the Spirit and belief in the truth

Hebrews 10:10 – We have been sanctified: through the offering of the body of Jesus Christ once for all

Hebrews 10:14 – We are sanctified: and perfected forever by His single offering

Hebrews 13:12 – We are sanctified: through Jesus' own blood

1 Peter 1:2 – We are sanctified: of the Spirit

Sanctification is the will of God (1 Thessalonians 4:3). Believing the truth of our sanctification is the inner healing process.

Let's look at two Scriptures about the kingdom of God and the definitions of two Greek words to help us understand why we pursue healing.

For the kingdom of God is not a matter of eating and drinking but of righteousness and peace and joy in the Holy Spirit. – Romans 14:17

But seek first the kingdom of God and His righteousness, and all these things will be added to you. – Matthew 6:33

Seek – the Greek word used here is *zēteō* (Strong's G2212). It means: to seek (literally or figuratively), worship God, be about, go about, desire, endeavor, enquire for, require, seek after, seek for.

First – the Greek word used here is *proton* (Strong's G4412). It means: firstly (in time, place, order, or importance), before, at the beginning, chiefly, first, first of all.

An expression of those two Scriptures including the fullness of those definitions could be:

> *Worship God by being about, going about, desiring, endeavoring for, enquiring for, requiring, and seeking His kingdom of righteousness, peace, and joy first, at the beginning, in the first order of importance, before anything else, and all these things will be added to you.*

The kingdom of God is righteousness, peace, and joy. We are called to seek these first. Intentionally seeking righteousness, peace, and joy is the will of God, and is what the Identity Restoration lifestyle is all about.

Here are a few specific Scriptures that help demonstrate the godly principle of seeking righteousness, peace, and joy.

RIGHTEOUSNESS

Matthew 5:6 – Blessed are those who hunger and thirst for righteousness, they will be satisfied

Matthew 6:33 – Seek first His righteousness

Romans 1:17 – Righteousness is revealed in the gospel

Romans 1:17 – The righteous will live by faith

Romans 5:17 – Receive righteousness

Romans 6:13,19 – Present yourself to God as righteous

Romans 14:17 – Righteousness is in the Holy Spirit

Ephesians 4:24 – Put on the new self, created after the likeness of God in true righteousness

Ephesians 6:14 – Put on the breastplate of righteousness

1 Timothy 6:11 – Pursue righteousness

2 Timothy 2:22 – Pursue righteousness

PEACE

John 20:21 – Peace be with you

Acts 16:36 – Go in peace

Romans 1:7 – Grace to you and peace from God our Father and the Lord Jesus Christ

Romans 5:1 – We have peace

Romans 14:19 – Pursue what makes for peace

Romans 15:13 – May God fill you with peace in believing

2 Corinthians 13:11 – Live in peace

Ephesians 2:14 – Jesus Himself is our peace

Ephesians 4:3 – Be eager to maintain unity by the bond of peace

Colossians 3:15 – Let the peace of Christ rule in your hearts

1 Thessalonians 5:13 – Be at peace

1 Timothy 2:2 – Lead a peaceful life

2 Timothy 2:22 – Pursue peace

Hebrews 12:14 – Strive for peace

James 3:17 – Peace is the wisdom of God

James 3:18 – Righteousness is sown in peace by those who make peace

1 Peter 1:2 – May peace be multiplied to you

1 Peter 3:11 – Seek peace and pursue it

2 Peter 1:2 – May peace be multiplied to you in the knowledge of God

2 Peter 3:14 – Be diligent to be found at peace

JOY

Matthew 25:21,23 – Enter into the joy

Luke 6:23 – Rejoice and leap for joy

John 15:10-11 – Abide in love that your joy may be full

John 16:24 – Ask and receive that your joy may be full

John 17:13 – Have His joy fulfilled in you

Romans 15:13 – Be filled with joy in believing

2 Corinthians 1:24 – Work with each other for our joy

James 1:2 – Count it all joy

An expression of all these Scriptures could be:

Seek, live by, put on, pursue, go in, have, be filled with, strive for, enter into, receive, and be diligent to be found in righteousness, peace, and joy.

In Chapter Two, we looked at the kingdom principle that the Holy Spirit glorifies Jesus by revealing to us the truth of who we are.

When the Spirit of truth comes, He will guide you into all the truth, for He will not speak on His own authority, but whatever He hears He will speak, and He will declare to you the things that are to come. He will glorify Me, for He will take what is Mine and declare it to you. All that the Father has is Mine; therefore I said that He will take what is Mine and declare it to you. – John 16:13-15

Pursuing the truth with the Holy Spirit, repenting from the lies, and believing the truth of who we are in Christ brings glory to Jesus. Pursuing healing glorifies Jesus.

But thanks be to God, that you who were once slaves of sin have become obedient from the heart to the standard of teaching to which you were committed, and, having been set free from sin, have become slaves of righteousness. – Romans 6:17-18

We pursue inner healing because our hearts are obedient and it brings glory to God.

PRACTICAL APPLICATION

For this practical application, we are going to categorize our lives and think about the kingdom of God in those areas.

Take a moment, and think about the different aspects of your life. There are some basic aspects that are the same for everybody, and then there are some perspectives and aspects that will be unique for you. Please, don't look up how to do this and copy something. This part of the process, of you thinking about and categorizing your life, is helpful in understanding yourself better. There is no wrong answer or wrong way to do this.

If you are ready, invite God into this process with you, and consider how you would categorize the different aspects of your life, and list them below. There is no magic number for this. Twelve blanks are provided, but you could have less or more.

_____   _____   _____

_____   _____   _____

_____   _____   _____

_____   _____   _____

As I coach people, the categories they have will sometimes change or expand during the process. Allow yourself to just start with whatever you have.

Now that we have the categories, we are going to rate the different aspects. Again, there are twelve blanks, but you could have more or less.

Transfer your list, one at a time, and rate each aspect in how you think or feel you are experiencing righteousness (R), peace (P), and joy (J) in each area. We will rate them from 1 to 10 in each category, with 1 being the least, and 10 being the most fulfilled in that area. So, if you are not experiencing righteousness in that category, you would have a lower number. If you are experiencing a lot of peace in that area, you would have a higher number. Go with your first gut reaction on each one. Please don't think too hard on these.

R	1-2-3-4-5-6-7-8-9-10	R	1-2-3-4-5-6-7-8-9-10
P	1-2-3-4-5-6-7-8-9-10	P	1-2-3-4-5-6-7-8-9-10
J	1-2-3-4-5-6-7-8-9-10	J	1-2-3-4-5-6-7-8-9-10

R	1-2-3-4-5-6-7-8-9-10	R	1-2-3-4-5-6-7-8-9-10
P	1-2-3-4-5-6-7-8-9-10	P	1-2-3-4-5-6-7-8-9-10
J	1-2-3-4-5-6-7-8-9-10	J	1-2-3-4-5-6-7-8-9-10

R	1-2-3-4-5-6-7-8-9-10	R	1-2-3-4-5-6-7-8-9-10
P	1-2-3-4-5-6-7-8-9-10	P	1-2-3-4-5-6-7-8-9-10
J	1-2-3-4-5-6-7-8-9-10	J	1-2-3-4-5-6-7-8-9-10

R	1-2-3-4-5-6-7-8-9-10	R	1-2-3-4-5-6-7-8-9-10
P	1-2-3-4-5-6-7-8-9-10	P	1-2-3-4-5-6-7-8-9-10
J	1-2-3-4-5-6-7-8-9-10	J	1-2-3-4-5-6-7-8-9-10

R	1-2-3-4-5-6-7-8-9-10		R	1-2-3-4-5-6-7-8-9-10
P	1-2-3-4-5-6-7-8-9-10		P	1-2-3-4-5-6-7-8-9-10
J	1-2-3-4-5-6-7-8-9-10		J	1-2-3-4-5-6-7-8-9-10

R	1-2-3-4-5-6-7-8-9-10		R	1-2-3-4-5-6-7-8-9-10
P	1-2-3-4-5-6-7-8-9-10		P	1-2-3-4-5-6-7-8-9-10
J	1-2-3-4-5-6-7-8-9-10		J	1-2-3-4-5-6-7-8-9-10

This is just a snapshot of how you are experiencing the kingdom of God in your life right now. Anywhere that you are experiencing less of the kingdom, it is absolutely possible to be more free.

Now that you have this information, let's pray and dream. Again, invite the Lord to help you with this. Think about the areas of your life where you had low numbers, and ask God these questions.

Ask God: *"When I experience more of the kingdom in these areas, how will that affect my life, and what will that be like?"*

Ask God: *"What are some practical steps I can take to experience more of the kingdom in my life?"*

_____

_____

_____

_____

Now ask the Holy Spirit to empower you and guide you in these steps.

This is one of the tools that I use in Identity Coaching to get a kingdom snapshot of people's lives. I have found this tool to be very helpful in establishing a starting point for the coaching process. For more information about coaching, visit our Faith by Grace[2] ministry page.

Endnotes:

1.   faithbygrace.org/resources
2.   faithbygrace.org

CHAPTER ELEVEN

LIVING FREE

N ow that we have explored the various aspects of the Identity Restoration lifestyle and are willing to be honest with ourselves, we can apply it to our lives and truly live free.

Let's take a moment and review. The truth of who we are is already true. We have been completely set free from sin, have become slaves to righteousness, and have the righteous requirement of the law fulfilled in us. We have been delivered from the kingdom of fear, shame, and guilt and transferred into the kingdom of righteousness, peace, and joy in the Holy Spirit. We can be emotionally and mentally present, choose reality, and experience the presence of God in our lives. We can take inventory of our hearts, by discovering the truth of who we are, the lies we are believing, the self-protections we are using, and the promises that are available to us. We are able to forgive, repent, and choose truth. We are no longer stuck in the details of our past, and we are able to be free from any demonic oppression.

This is an Identity Restoration lifestyle, and it is our guaranteed inheritance in Christ. This lifestyle of intentionally pursuing the truth, without denying what might be happening in our hearts, is obedience to the Word and is life giving. Just stop and think about that for a minute. Jesus did all of that for us!

Let's start by examining what it looks like to live that way. First, remember that righteousness, peace, and joy are normal. This is what our lives are able to be filled with, regardless of our circumstances, and that is what we are pursuing.

One of the simplest ways to live free is to focus on, and be grateful for, the goodness that we have in Christ.

> Do not be anxious about anything, but in everything by prayer and supplication with thanksgiving let your requests be made known to God. And the peace of God, which surpasses all understanding, will guard your hearts and your minds in Christ Jesus. Finally, brothers, whatever is true, whatever is honorable, whatever is just, whatever is pure, whatever is lovely, whatever is commendable, if there is any excellence, if there is anything worthy of praise, think about these things. – Philippians 4:6-8

Focusing on and celebrating everything that is true, honorable, just, pure, lovely, commendable, excellent, and praiseworthy is such an incredible way to experience freedom.

Remember from Chapter Ten that we are seeking, living by, putting on, pursuing, going in, having, being filled with, striving for, entering into, receiving, and being diligent to be found in righteousness, peace, and joy.

Here are some fun Scriptures I found, for your enjoyment, that describe this lifestyle:

In his days may the righteous flourish, and peace abound, till the moon be no more! – Psalm 72:7

Steadfast love and faithfulness meet; righteousness and peace kiss each other. – Psalm 85:10

The hope of the righteous brings joy. – Proverbs 10:28

But the righteous shall be glad; they shall exult before God; they shall be jubilant with joy! – Psalm 68:3

Those who plan peace have joy. – Proverbs 12:20b

And the effect of righteousness will be peace, and the result of righteousness, quietness and trust forever. – Isaiah 32:17

Oh that you had paid attention to My commandments! Then your peace would have been like a river, and your righteousness like the waves of the sea. – Isaiah 48:18

I will make your overseers peace and your taskmasters righteousness. – Isaiah 60:17b

Peace I leave with you; My peace I give to you. Not as the world gives do I give to you. Let not your hearts be troubled, neither let them be afraid. – John 14:27

May the God of hope fill you with all joy and peace in believing, so that by the power of the Holy Spirit you may abound in hope. – Romans 15:13

You have loved righteousness and hated wickedness; therefore God, your God, has anointed you with the oil of gladness beyond your companions. – Hebrews 1:9

And a harvest of righteousness is sown in peace by those who make peace. – James 3:18

This is what our normal life in Christ can be like:

Righteousness flourishing

Peace abounding

Steadfast love and faithfulness meeting

Righteousness and peace kissing

Righteous hope bringing joy

Glad exultation before God

Jubilance with joy

Peaceful, effective righteousness

Quietness and trust resulting from righteousness

Rivers of peace

Waves of righteousness like the sea

Peace as an overseer

Righteousness as a taskmaster

Untroubled, fearless peace

Filled with all peace and joy in believing

Abounding in hope

Loving righteousness

Anointed with gladness

Having a harvest of righteousness sown in peace

Just meditate on that for a few minutes. Read through it again and again, until it stirs you. Let your hunger arise for righteousness, peace, and joy and be satisfied.

When that righteousness, peace, and joy is not what is happening and we find ourselves experiencing fear, shame, and guilt, we have the permission, confidence, power, and authority, in the Word of God, to acknowledge it, capture the thoughts, make them obedient to Christ, and pursue the kingdom of God. We are now equipped and empowered to be able to choose life. The Lord has given us the freedom of choice.

> I call heaven and earth to witness against you today, that
> I have set before you life and death, blessing and curse.
> Therefore choose life, that you and your offspring may live.
> – Deuteronomy 30:19

A lifestyle of freedom involves choice. The Lord has given us freedom to choose what kingdom we live in. We can choose the kingdom of the world, and hide in fear, cover ourselves in shame, and blame out of guilt. Or, we can choose the kingdom of God, and live in the authority of our peace, joyfully accepting our identity, and being in right relationship with ourselves, God, and our community.

And again He said, "To what shall I compare the kingdom of God? It is like leaven that a woman took and hid in three measures of flour, until it was all leavened." – Luke 13:20-21

"We are perfect in Christ, but we are not perfectly living out who we are in Christ."

The fullness of the kingdom is increasing in us like the leaven in Luke 13. The kingdom of God is already in us; we just don't always fully represent that kingdom. This understanding, that we are not fully mature in Christ, will help us live free. We are perfect in Christ, but we are not perfectly living out who we are in Christ. We don't have the years of experience of trusting God in the areas of our lives where we were believing lies and self-protecting. As we get set free from these lies, there is a maturing that needs to happen in our hearts. Immaturity in itself is not a sin. It is just a lack of experience and understanding. Accepting that we don't know it all, and that we need to mature, will help us to be able to mature. The Word tells us in 2 Corinthians 3:18 that we are being transformed into the same image of God from one degree of glory to another. This represents the maturing and sanctification process. As we believe the truth of who we are in Christ, we will mature in our hearts, and begin to represent that truth, from one degree of glory to another.

Now the Lord is the Spirit, and where the Spirit of the Lord is, there is freedom. And we all, with unveiled face, beholding the glory of the Lord, are being transformed into the same image from one degree of glory to another. For this comes from the Lord who is the Spirit.
– 2 Corinthians 3:17-18

*"A life of glorious increase in the
representation of righteousness, peace,
and joy is the normal Christian life."*

We are maturing from one degree of glory to another in our identity, authority, and community. A life of glorious increase in the representation of righteousness, peace, and joy is the normal Christian life. This comes from the Lord, who is the Spirit, and where the Spirit of the Lord is, there is freedom. We are free to love God, love our neighbor, and love ourselves.

> "Teacher, which is the great commandment in the Law?" And He said to him, "You shall love the Lord your God with all your heart and with all your soul and with all your mind. This is the great and first commandment. And a second is like it: You shall love your neighbor as yourself. On these two commandments depend all the Law and the Prophets." – Matthew 22:36-40

Without righteousness, peace, and joy, we are unable to fulfill the great commandment and glorify the Lord. With them, we will innately love God, love our neighbor, and love ourselves, in the power of the Holy Spirit.

In Chapter Four we explored some possible ways the kingdom of the world could look in our lives. Now, let's look at how the kingdom of God could look in our lives.

This is the kingdom of God in the power of the Holy Spirit

Righteousness   Peace   Joy

This will directly affect your:

Community   Authority   Identity

This is what those effects can look like:

Relationships	Victory	Confidence
Togetherness	Understanding	Wisdom
Provision	Clarity	Purpose
Trust	Power	Acceptance
Affirmation	Vision	Hope
Able to give	Able to do	Able to receive

This is just a glimpse of what is available. There is so much more.

> But the fruit of the Spirit is love, joy, peace, patience, kindness, goodness, faithfulness, gentleness, self-control; against such things there is no law. And those who belong to Christ Jesus have crucified the flesh with its passions and desires. If we live by the Spirit, let us also keep in step with the Spirit. – Galatians 5:22-25

PRACTICAL APPLICATION

Let's just have some fun for this practical application. Let's review the Scriptures from earlier in the chapter and then make some statements of faith that we can express and declare with our voices.

Read each Scripture over yourself, and then declare the corresponding statements of faith. Let yourself enjoy this.

> In his days may the righteous flourish, and peace abound, till the moon be no more! – Psalm 72:7

"I will flourish in righteousness, and abound in peace, all the days of my life."

> Steadfast love and faithfulness meet; righteousness and peace kiss each other. – Psalm 85:10

"God's steadfast love and faithfulness meet me right where His righteousness and peace kiss."

> The hope of the righteous brings joy. – Proverbs 10:28

"God has made me righteous, and my hope brings joy."

> But the righteous shall be glad; they shall exult before God; they shall be jubilant with joy! – Psalm 68:3

"I am glad, and I can express jubilant exultation before God, with joy!"

> Those who plan peace have joy. – Proverbs 12:20b

"I plan peace, and I have joy."

> And the effect of righteousness will be peace, and the result of righteousness, quietness and trust forever. – Isaiah 32:17

"God's righteousness produces peace in my life, and the result of His righteous peace is quietness and trust forever."

Oh that you had paid attention to My commandments! Then your peace would have been like a river, and your righteousness like the waves of the sea. – Isaiah 48:18

"My heart is attentive to the commandments of God. My peace is like a river, and my righteousness is like the waves of the sea."

I will make your overseers peace and your taskmasters righteousness. – Isaiah 60:17b

"Peace oversees and manages my life. Righteousness is my driver and ruler."

Peace I leave with you; My peace I give to you. Not as the world gives do I give to you. Let not your hearts be troubled, neither let them be afraid. – John 14:27

"My heart is not troubled or afraid. Jesus has given me His peace, and His peace remains."

May the God of hope fill you with all joy and peace in believing, so that by the power of the Holy Spirit you may abound in hope. – Romans 15:13

"The God of hope fills me with all joy and peace in believing. The power of the Holy Spirit causes me to abound in hope."

You have loved righteousness and hated wickedness;

therefore God, your God, has anointed you with the oil of gladness beyond your companions. – Hebrews 1:9

"I love righteousness, and my God has anointed me with the oil of gladness."

And a harvest of righteousness is sown in peace by those who make peace. – James 3:18

"I am a peacemaker, and I have a harvest of righteousness that has been sown in peace."

CHAPTER TWELVE

WHAT NOW?

What do you do now that you have all of this information and know how to live a practical and sustainable lifestyle of freedom?

"Be still, and know that I am God. I will be exalted among the nations, I will be exalted in the earth!" The LORD of hosts is with us; the God of Jacob is our fortress.
– Psalm 46:10-11

Be calm and know that God is God. You don't have to figure it all out, rush, or hurry through this. Patience is a fruit of the Spirit, and He is patient with us. In all the encounters I have experienced with the Lord, personally, or in sessions, I have never seen Him worried, rushed, or in a hurry. Jesus is always peaceful, Father God is always right on time, and the Holy Spirit is always finding a way to make things right.

With faith as the motivator, there will be actual changes in your life as you believe the truth. There will be changes in your thought processes, your behaviors, and your habits.

In the same way, faith by itself, if it is not accompanied by action, is dead. – James 2:17

You see that his faith and his actions were working together, and his faith was made complete by what he did.
– James 2:22

Your faith will cause you to act, and the actions in your life will reveal and complete your faith. If your actions and your life don't match what you think you believe, it may be worth testing to see what you do actually believe.

There are many tactics of discouragement the enemy will use to keep us from pursuing a lifestyle of freedom. Two common areas of focus are timing and amount. I see this cause people to think things like: "It's too late for me to pursue healing," or "My sin is too much." These are just two examples of what I have seen – there are many variations of those lies. The Word tells us in 2 Corinthians 2:11 that we are not ignorant of the enemy's designs. Trying to get you to think that it is not the right time to pursue healing, or that your sin is somehow too much for Jesus to handle, are two of the enemy's designs. It is never too late to discover the truth of who you are in Christ. It is never the wrong time to repent and believe the gospel. Jesus was made to be sin so that we could become the righteousness of God. He took up all of our sin. There is no sin that He is not already aware of in your life.

"Your faith will cause you to act, and the actions in your life will reveal and complete your faith."

For our sake He made Him to be sin who knew no sin, so

that in Him we might become the righteousness of God.
– 2 Corinthians 5:21

For then He would have had to suffer repeatedly since the foundation of the world. But as it is, He has appeared once for all at the end of the ages to put away sin by the sacrifice of Himself. And just as it is appointed for man to die once, and after that comes judgment, so Christ, having been offered once to bear the sins of many, will appear a second time, not to deal with sin but to save those who are eagerly waiting for Him. – Hebrews 9:26-28

He is the propitiation for our sins, and not for ours only but also for the sins of the whole world. – 1 John 2:2

Bear – the Greek word used here is *anapherō* (Strong's G630). It means: to take up, bear, bring up, carry up, lead up, offer up.

An expression of these Scriptures including the fullness of this definition could be:

> *For our sake He made Jesus to be sin who knew no sin. He was offered once to take up, bear, bring up, carry up, lead up, and offer up our sins. He is the propitiation for our sins, and not for ours only but also for the sins of the whole world, so that in Him we might become the righteousness of God.*

Not only was Jesus made to be sin, but He bore all of our sins and carried them up. He is the propitiation for our sins. He is familiar with all of our sins. He already knows every thought, action, or behavior you have ever had. There is nothing you have done that Jesus doesn't already know.

O Lord, you have searched me and known me! You know when I sit down and when I rise up; you discern my thoughts from afar. You search out my path and my lying down and are acquainted with all my ways. Even before a word is on my tongue, behold, O Lord, You know it altogether. You hem me in, behind and before, and lay Your hand upon me. Such knowledge is too wonderful for me; it is high; I cannot attain it. Where shall I go from Your Spirit? Or where shall I flee from Your presence? – Psalm 139:1-7

No secret is hidden from You. – Ezekiel 28:3b

"Can a man hide himself in secret places so that I cannot see him? declares the Lord. Do I not fill heaven and earth? declares the LORD." – Jeremiah 23:24

Not only does Jesus know about everything, He has already supplied more than enough grace for whatever amount of sin we have.

Now the law came in to increase the trespass, but where sin increased, grace abounded all the more, so that, as sin reigned in death, grace also might reign through righteousness leading to eternal life through Jesus Christ our Lord. – Romans 5:20-21

And God is able to make all grace abound to you, so that having all sufficiency in all things at all times, you may abound in every good work. – 2 Corinthians 9:8

Pursuing the kingdom through a lifestyle of freedom and healing is a good work. God will supply all the grace you need for it. You don't need to do it in your own effort. He will make His presence known to you anywhere you are willing to meet Him, and He will supply all the grace you need.

> Come to Me, all who labor and are heavy laden, and I will give you rest. Take My yoke upon you, and learn from Me, for I am gentle and lowly in heart, and you will find rest for your souls. For My yoke is easy, and My burden is light.
> – Matthew 11:28-30

There are some practical resources and next steps that I can recommend for you to consider. As you consider these, allow yourself to act in faith as the Lord prompts you.

RECOMMENDATIONS

The first step I would recommend is to start applying the principles and concepts from this book into your life. Just applying the "Three Steps to Life" will drastically impact your freedom. Simply allowing yourself to be present and to experience the presence of God, in your reality, will soon transform your experiences into His reality.

As you apply the Identity Restoration principles to your life, and you find some areas that you can't resolve, consider getting help. Remember

"Simply allowing yourself to be present and to experience the presence of God, in your reality, will soon transform your experience into His reality."

from James 5:16, we are to confess our sins to each other and pray for each other, so that we may be healed.

There are many options for help. Your local church may already have a process set up. I would recommend checking with your pastor or a trusted leader for counsel. If you cannot get resolution through that, I would recommend reaching out to other trusted places. One of those is the *Bethel Sozo* network.[1] There you can find local ministers who can help you encounter truth.

My wife Kathryn and I are the co-leaders of *Faith by Grace Ministries*.[2] We equip people for a lifestyle of freedom through Identity Discovery Sessions, Identity Coaching, workshops, and conferences. You can find out more about us on our website. We can meet with you personally if we are in your area, or you could meet with a member of our team. We also do skype sessions with people all around the world.

There are also some tangible products to help you pursue freedom. These are some of the resources that I believe may be beneficial to your journey:

Who Do You Think You Are? Bible Study, Volume One[3] – Ray Leight

First, I would recommend my Bible Study Workbook, *Who Do You Think You Are?* This is one of the most comprehensive resources available to discover your identity in Christ, and to be transformed into that truth. You will have the opportunity to read through hundreds of Scriptures, in context, and get revelation of over 250 different aspects of your identity in Christ. It focuses on your redeemed, alive, righteous, fruitful, pure, and accepted identity in Christ.

Who Do You Think You Are? Devotional, Volume One[3] – Ray Leight

This 21-Day Devotional will give you the chance to daily review the truth of who God says you are, and then process your thoughts and beliefs to help you align with His truth. This devotional focuses on your redeemed, alive, righteous, fruitful, pure, and accepted identity in Christ.

TrueFaced[4] – Thrall, McNicol, Lynch

TrueFaced draws a clear distinction between two very different underlying motives Christians sometimes operate under: our determination to please God or to trust Him. This book shows us how to trust Him more. Explore issues of identity and grace in your relationships with others and with God.

The Healing Presence[5] – Leanne Payne

This is one of Leanne Payne's foundational books that explains the basis of her counseling ministry that allows the presence and power of Jesus to bring healing into wounded lives.

Hearing 101[6] – Faith Blatchford

Hearing 101 is a short, practical book that teaches the reader how to hear God's voice. We were created to have intimate communication with our Heavenly Father. God will talk to anyone who will listen. Our hearing problem is not from God's side, but rather from ours. This book uncovers the lies and fears that block us from hearing.

Shifting Atmospheres[7] – Dawna De Silva

The idea behind this book is to help you learn which issues you will face internally and which ones you will treat as broadcasts of the enemy. The exercises included are aimed at training your senses to discern what is good and what is evil. Dawna's hope is that you start learning how to stand in authority over both your own soul (what goes on internally) and the schemes of the enemy (what goes on externally).

Sozo[8] – Teresa Liebscher, Dawna De Silva

The Biblical concept of salvation comes from the Greek word 'Sozo' and has a holistic implication. Power and victory flowed through the New Testament Church because the early Christians understood how to live out their salvation in a way that impacted every area of their lives—spirit, soul, and body. In *Sozo*, Dawna DeSilva and Teresa Liebscher provide revelatory teaching and miraculous testimonies that paint a stunning picture of how to experience Heaven's freedom in every area of your life.

Money and the Prosperous Soul[9] - Stephen De Silva

This book is pivotal in helping you discover and break free from an orphan, victim mentality and a poverty mindset. In a warm, conversational style, Stephen combines practical financial teaching with sound biblical truth. Discover the supernatural keys to breaking free from destructive financial cycles.

Winning the Battle for the Night[6] – Faith Blatchford

In our fast-paced world, we see sleep as "wasted time," or else we lie awake as anxiety, fear, or distractions run through our minds. That was never God's intent for the night. Without realizing it, we've handed this sacred time over to the enemy. With warmth, compassion, and keen biblical insight, counselor and speaker Faith Blatchford reveals that it's during this precious time that God imparts everything necessary for us to be equipped for the day. Without peaceful sleep at night, we are robbed mentally, physically, emotionally, and spiritually of the resources we need.

Thank you for taking the time to read through this book. I truly believe your life will be transformed by applying the principles and concepts in these chapters.

> May the God of hope fill you with all joy and peace in believing, so that by the power of the Holy Spirit you may abound in hope. – Romans 15:13

Blessings,

Ray Leight

Endnotes:

1. bethelsozo.com
2. faithbygrace.org
3. faithbygrace.org/resources
4. trueface.org
5. ministriesofpastoralcare.com
6. faithblatchford.com
7. dawnadesilva.com
8. bethelsozo.com
9. stephenkdesilva.com

TESTIMONIES

GORDON'S STORY

I came in for an Inner Healing Session with Ray because I was not handling certain things well. I was very angry and becoming verbally confrontational. I was diagnosed as bipolar by my psychologist. I liked the highs, but the lows were becoming life threatening (to me). After my session, I experienced immediate healing.

At first, I was afraid I would lose the creativity that came with the highs, but this did not happen. I still have a large, perhaps better, creative capacity. But now I don't get the lows. A side effect of that is that I no longer procrastinate to get things done until I have an emotional high. I also find that I am no longer angry most of the time.

The peace I am experiencing now is amazing. I have directly seen the benefits of this healing playing out in my emotions over the past two years.

I no longer experience the symptoms of the bipolar diagnosis.

I am so much more productive now. I am more able to appropriately interact with people, and my relationship with God continues to deepen.

RANDALL'S STORY

I came in for an Identity Healing Session because of a major career transition and we had recently become empty nesters. I was dealing with a lack of a sense of where God was leading me and what impact I could make for His kingdom.

During the session I experienced a loving, gentle side of Jesus, rather than the judging and punishment side I had grown up relating to. I was able to let go of some of the past mistakes I had made and put them behind me once and for all. Seeing Jesus taking these away from me and paying for my freedom was very powerful.

Since the Identity Session, I now find that I am more forgiving of myself and others. I am less judgmental and more willing to admit my mistakes to others. I do not see God as only a judge waiting to punish me, but as a loving father.

I see that even though I am broken, I just need to be available for God's power to work through me. Personally, I feel less hurried and less of a need to try and prove myself. I have a more personal relationship with God, not so structured and routine.

In my marriage, I find myself willing to express my concerns and to accept my issues and my wife's issues. We are growing in our faith together more than ever.

I am more forgiving with my family and more patient. I am looking for ways to grow closer rather than for issues to correct.

Relationships are now my focus, where in the past achieving goals was my main focus. Growing my relationships has taken on a new level of importance. I see my career more as a place to help others grow and less about achieving things for me.

I think that having time to focus on what issues are blocking a closer relationship with God and addressing those is something that anyone who is wanting to grow in their walk could benefit from. It gave me an understanding of what Jesus has done and is doing for me personally.

JONATHAN'S STORY

I came in for an Identity Healing Session because there were a number of emotional and relational habits I had been working on to bring health to, for the last 10 years, and had finally hit the end of what I was able to do on my own. I realized I needed some outside help to unlock some deeply held beliefs that were keeping me from experiencing love in many key areas of my life.

I was dealing with high levels of co-dependency that were affecting all my relationships in my life, in one way or another. I had feelings of not being present in my life and not being able to show up and be really intimate. I think at the core of all that, I wasn't able to really hear my own heart and be myself without constantly feeling like I was drowning under the weight of all the shoulds of shame.

In the session I could feel core beliefs shifting and changing, which was rather uncomfortable at times as these were foundational pieces of my perception of myself. So there were definitely weeks of feeling like I was untethered, which was really scary and unnerving at times. I didn't know who I was or what I really believed any more. My faith had been built on decades of performance and shame, and without that I didn't know if I had a faith anymore. I had to rediscover myself and let myself revert to more immature behaviors for a while to let my heart reset and grow to be motivated from freedom instead of the shame and guilt.

I have received so much healing and freedom it's hard to know where to start. I can hear my heart. For one of the first times in my life I can consistently hear the desires of my heart. I had no idea how much of my life was dictated by guilt and "shoulds", but now I can just do the things that I want. I can do the dishes because I want to, not because I should or have to, and by doing it because I want to, I am so much more present and by extension joyful. I'm no longer living under the tyranny of my own agenda, constantly missing the enjoyment of the moment because I am trying to make it better or plan for the next thing. I feel like I am finally the true self I could always see but never discipline myself into becoming. Now it just flows out of me, life and love and joy. I no longer feel I am missing my kid's childhoods, but just being in it with them.

I can trust the desires of my heart now. Now when I don't want to do the things I should, I trust my heart will get me where I need to go. It may seem less direct, but it's actually the opposite because I will be present in all the things I am doing rather than ALWAYS wishing I was doing something else.

There is a stunning difference in my relationships now. I grew up codependent, constantly gauging every relational interaction to figure out what the other people wanted from me in a given situation and then trying to perform up to that expectation. And always falling short of my own judgement, because it was vague and impossible to begin with. But now I am able see it when it comes up and readjust to a goal of just being present.

The fear is nearly gone. In my career I was constantly afraid I wasn't measuring up, because I never met my own self imagined expectations from my co-workers and superiors. Now I can be confident and do better work. More than that, now I enjoy my work because I show up and I am able to be myself in it.

I have recommended this to numerous people and at least three of them have had sessions with Ray as a result. Ray's style and approach is one of the most effective I have seen because it is so simple and lends itself so easily to transitioning to normal life. I couldn't help but learn how to do it with myself during the course of my sessions. As a result, I am empowered to continue bringing healthfulness and love into the areas of my life that need it without being dependent on Ray for it. Rather, I can use him as an asset to help unlock those particularly stubborn areas in my heart. I am immensely grateful for my time with Ray and would recommend him to anyone who feels like they can't access their true selves.

ADAM'S STORY

I have had an incredible experience with deep inner healing guidance with Kathryn. We have worked together for several months and immediately God's love has worked through her to reach deep healing and revelations of God's love for me in every circumstance in my life. Kathryn has worked at a pace that has been consistent with my heart's need for safety and comfort through a difficult time in my life. God has showed up in each session and it's been amazing. This has been a true gift to also work with Kathryn for coaching in many areas of my life. As a business owner in the entertainment industry in Los Angeles, I seek guidance that's in alignment with my passion to also serve and steward God's blessings and this has been very helpful.

I've also had the pleasure of working in great detail through the *Who Do You Think You Are?* Bible study which has formed a great picture and understanding of our righteousness through faith that I have not found elsewhere. I highly recommend this and have ordered this study for others. It's been excellent. Thank you!

ELIJAH'S STORY

Ray's coaching impressed me in several ways. It was very different from other inner healing and prayer ministry that I have experienced. First, it was not about digging up the dark details of my past. Instead, it felt surprisingly gentle. Second, was the results. I noticed that things that used to trigger me, no longer did. Lastly, it was a great balance between being real and honest with listening to the Holy Spirit.

JACK'S STORY

I came in for an Identity Coaching Session because I wanted to go after some issues that had been long-standing, and different approaches hadn't really seen much success.

I was dealing with issues of performance, self-doubt, and shame at failure. During the session I felt I got a real insight into the roots of some of my struggles. Since the session I have definitely felt a "lift" from the need to perform, and shame when my performance isn't great. I am less introspective in a self-critical way. I also feel I have much more peace and confidence, and worry less.

I definitely recommend this. Understanding roots can reveal information that can make the difference between freedom or not.

SUZIE'S STORY

I had been receiving life coaching and we kept running into an issue that led my life coach to refer me to Ray for an Inner Healing

Session. The Lord has had me on a journey of identity – discovering who I am and embracing all of me. But I started to realize that I had what I would call an internal Evaluator who was watching and critiquing my every move. I was nervous about going for inner healing again because I felt like I had "failed" at it in the past! But with Ray somehow every part of who I am got validated! My Evaluator and all my protective mechanisms were accepted and affirmed and then redeemed. This is what I later wrote in my journal: "I wasn't a problem; I wasn't too difficult; I wasn't an embarrassment. All of me – even scared me, protective me, blank me, evaluating me, confused me – all of me was valid, was accepted, was seen and understood – was okay. I wasn't bad – I was okay. I was ALL okay!" I left feeling hopeful, lighter, wondrous – free. Finally embracing me because the Father and Jesus and the Holy Spirit were fully embracing me! It was absolutely amazing!!

I have continued to walk in this healing – it was a huge turning point in my life! I am free now to actually discover and embrace who I am because I no longer have a critical Evaluator judging every thought or action – I don't live in that fear anymore. I have experienced my heart being fully embraced by God so I am able to pay attention to and care for my heart as well! I get to be fully me! I can't put words to how amazing that is! I am experiencing more and more freedom in all my relationships – I get to love and not be afraid. I walk in so much more confidence and joy and freedom! I would encourage anyone who wants to experience a deep healing in their heart and identity to meet with Ray! My life will never be the same again!

I started going through the *Who Do You Think You Are?* Bible study after my Inner Healing Session with Ray. It was an excellent way to lean into the healing that God had brought to me through our session. In the note at the beginning, Ray says, "This life-changing study will allow you to discover who you are, how to accept yourself, and what it looks like to live out the truth of who God created you to be." This is TRUE!!! This is an incredibly powerful study because Ray combines

Scripture study with actively inviting the Holy Spirit to reveal the truth of what God is saying personally to you and to reveal any thoughts or feelings you have that don't actually line up with what Scripture is saying. Then asking God to uncover the lies you are believing and walk through forgiveness, breaking agreement with the lies and receiving what Jesus wants to give us instead, then declaring the truths that God has revealed to you. I had huge moments of breakthrough going through this study as the Holy Spirit revealed what I actually believed and then led me through changing those beliefs! I have declarations on my wall that the Lord spoke into my heart in the study. Rhema words from the Lord based soundly in Scripture – His logos Word. I recommend this Bible Study to everyone! Even after completing a year of ministry school which is all about identity, this study took it to an entirely new level for me and really solidified the truth of who I am in Christ which affects every aspect of my life!

SHANNON'S STORY

I have been to an Identity Restoration Workshop, gone through the *Who Do You Think You Are?* Devotional, and have experienced Inner Healing Identity Sessions.

I was seeking ministry because I was hungry to grow and experience the Father's love and know His heart. I was dealing with feelings of hopelessness and mediocrity. I was lifeless and bored with my life as a Christian, and had the inability to experience deeper levels of intimacy.

During the ministry times I received FREEEEEEEDOOOOOOM! I received the confidence that I hear from God. I experienced the most profound, life-changing, deepest level of God's love for me.

EVERYTHING IS DIFFERENT NOW! I will never be the same! I have broken free of a religious mindset that kept joy and peace from being a reality in my life. I know who I am and whose I am, and I am able to foster the freedom I experience within my home, with my husband, and with my kids, creating deep levels of intimacy.

I would recommend this, and I do! All the time, just in sharing my testimony. Freedom is contagious and my life will honestly never be the same. I am eternally grateful for this ministry, for new levels of hope, deeper intimacy with Jesus, and purpose for my life.

KEN'S STORY

The reason I came in for an Inner Healing Identity Session is because I was experiencing shame, incapacitating fear, and the fear of death.

I expected that my ministry times with Ray would be beneficial because I had heard raving recommendations about him. I have had many counseling, deliverance, and inner healing ministry sessions in my lifetime. And, I have been transformed by those sessions—men and women partnering with God to offer greater freedom/wholeness to me. But what I didn't expect was the intensity with which God personally tended to me in my sessions with Ray. All of life and earth faded away as God shocked me with His leadership, His answers, His encouragement, and His correction. And, I walked away with Ray's notes outlining what God had said and done inside of me. Ray's gift is unique. My ability to deal with those life challenges is radically different today. I'm so grateful that Ray was available when I needed help.

I absolutely recommend a session with Ray because it was transformational for me. I encountered God profoundly. And, I had the ability to not allow my fears/symptoms to dominate me after meeting with Ray.

JUSTIN'S STORY

I first met with Ray and Kathryn because I had been feeling distant from God and wanted to be closer to Him. I wanted an increased intimacy with Jesus and a closer relationship with the Holy Spirit. I wanted to talk to Him and hear from Him during my days.

For a long time, I did not know (or believe) my identity as a beloved child of God. I "knew" that God loved me but did not really believe it in my heart. I wrestled with fear, uncertainty, and insecurity. I did not have a clear sense of myself and constantly doubted my decision making. Because I was so unhappy with, and unsure of, myself, my relationship with my family, friends, and even my wife and children felt strained and tense at times.

Though I did not know Ray and Kathryn previously, I experienced intimate interaction with the Father and with Jesus while praying with them. The Holy Spirit spoke to me and God told me what He thought of me, how He loves me, and who He's made me to be.

Through the encouragement of wonderful brothers and sisters like Ray and Kathryn, and through time with Jesus in prayer, I have received healing and freedom from my own insecurity and self-condemnation. I have become free to be who I am in Jesus – the beloved child of my Father in heaven! I am also free to see others according to who they are in the eyes of Jesus – and this gift has brought an incredible peace and contentment which had eluded me for most of my life.

I feel more peace today than I have in a long time and am continuing to experience the goodness and fullness of the life that is available in and with Jesus! I have a greater faith and greater joy in my life simply through the exercise of believing Jesus more – which, according to Him, is the work of God!

My wife and I have grown closer to God and each other as a result of learning to pray together and listen for God's voice and His leading in our lives. I can't tell you the gift it is to find that my wife has more patience and mercy for me – as I do for her.

My entire family, and even our friends and coworkers, have been blessed immeasurably through my wife and I becoming more aware of God's love for us. Having a greater understanding of God's love makes it very difficult to not feel empathy and a greater sense of mercy for others.

God has used Ray and Kathryn Leight powerfully to help me accept and believe Jesus about who He says I am. I cannot thank them enough for helping to impress these truths into my heart.

I highly recommend the *Who Do You Think You Are?* study, and any available time with Ray and Kathryn. The truths contained in the Scriptures outlined in this study, and in prayer, have been life-changing. My relationship with Jesus has grown in ways I could not have imagined!

VICTORIA'S STORY

I scheduled an Inner Healing Session with Ray. I had heard of the power and clarity received during these sessions and wanted to hear the voice of God. I had many childhood wounds that needed God's healing touch.

In the beginning of the session, I instantly began to get a clear picture, but very quickly lost the picture—everything went blurry. It seemed like nothing, but that was the first self-protecting system that was revealed during my time with Ray. I had been using this system for years to deal with pain and unwanted emotions.

I learned so many things about myself and God during that time. But if

I have to pick one moment that really stood out to me, it was realizing how deeply I believed the lie that I was alone. This mindset had such a negative effect on my life, my marriage, and my overall well-being. My husband works very odd hours and I'm alone most nights. I would find myself focusing on the fact that I was alone, not being driven to do my own passions because of the thick layer of depression it would bring.

During the session, when the "I'm Alone" came up, God told me I am never alone; He's always there with me to listen, laugh, or cry with. For the first time in my life I heard it and I believed it. This truth poured over my soul like purified water over dry, dusty hands.

When I came back home I recapped with my husband about my experience. My words brought tears to his eyes. He knew the deep pain and struggle I had been "maintaining" for the past 9 years. He was seeing them step into the light for the first time. I was on a high, floating on a cloud. I wondered how long this feeling would stay.

Two weeks later while I was in my kitchen, I got word that my husband would be working very late again. For the first time since my session, thoughts of aloneness and depression began to seep in. But this time something radically different happened. I felt the words that I heard from God in that room with Ray loud and clear. I physically felt the presence of God fill the kitchen and I began to weep tears of joy.

I actually believed I was not alone and that God was with me. I was shouting "I'm not alone! I'm not alone!" with tears of joy that soon turned to laughter. My mindset had completely flipped. I put on music and had a very productive night. This lie had no place in my heart!

Here I am two years later, and I am still very free from my old patterns of thought. From time to time I still chose to stay in the old thought pattern, but for the most part I choose to believe the truth that was revealed to me that day. I know I have the open invitation to tap into His presence of peace whenever I want. He's always there, I AM NOT ALONE, AND HE WILL NEVER LEAVE ME! I now enjoy the relationships I'm blessed with in a healthy way, not as a filler for the spot that God is supposed to fill. No person or thing can fill the space in me that was desperately thirsting for the Presence of my Father.

I'm so thankful to have met Ray and Kathryn and to call them friends to this day. Since then my husband has met with Ray, and many of our friends have as well. We have seen so many people touched by the ministry they're doing. Thank you so much Ray and Kathryn for your deep care and love for people. God bless your ministry abundantly.

Let these testimonies give you hope. What will be your story?

Freedom is available.

Made in the USA
Middletown, DE
27 November 2021

52984148R00089